MAY   2010

THE
POLITICS OF
HOPE
the WORDS OF
BARACK OBAMA

THE POLITICS OF HOPE
the WORDS OF BARACK OBAMA

Henry Russell

NH
NEW
HOLLAND

The author wishes to thank Meredith Jones Russell
and Jane Gaber for their help and advice.

First published in 2009 by New Holland Publishers (UK) Ltd
London • Cape Town • Sydney • Auckland
www.newhollandpublishers.com

10 9 8 7 6 5 4 3 2 1

Garfield House, 86–88 Edgware Road, London W2 2EA, UK
80 McKenzie Street, Cape Town 8001, South Africa
Unit 1, 66 Gibbes Street, Chatswood, NSW 2067, Australia
218 Lake Road, Northcote, Auckland, New Zealand

ISBN: 978 1 84773 507 2

Senior Editor: Kate Parker
Editorial Direction: Rosemary Wilkinson
Publisher: Aruna Vasudevan
Design and cover design: David Etherington
Production: Melanie Dowland

Printed and bound by Athenaeum Press Ltd, Gateshead, UK

NOTE: UK spellings are used throughout in this book, apart from for names.

Contents

Foreword
Charlotte Higgins

THE NEW CICERO

In the run-up to the US presidential election, the online magazine *Slate* ran a series of dictionary definitions of 'Obamaisms'. One ran thus: 'Barocrates (buh-ROH-cruh-teez) n. An obscure Greek philosopher who pioneered a method of teaching in which sensitive topics are first posed as questions then evaded'.

There were other digs at Barack Obama that alluded to ancient Greece and Rome. When he accepted the Democratic party nomination, he did so before a stagey backdrop of Doric columns. Republicans said this betrayed delusions of grandeur: this was a temple out of which Obama would emerge like a self-styled Greek god. (The *Guardian* cartoonist Steve Bell also discerned a Romanness in the image, and drew Obama as a toga-ed emperor.) In fact, the resonance of those pillars was much more complicated than the Republicans would have it. They recalled the White House, which itself summoned up visual echoes of the Roman republic, on whose constitution that of the US is based.

They recalled the Lincoln Memorial, before which
Martin Luther King delivered his 'I have a dream'
speech. They recalled the building on which the
Lincoln Memorial is based – the Parthenon. By
drawing us symbolically to Athens, we were located at
the very birthplace of democracy.

Here's the thing: to understand the next four years of
American politics, you are going to need to understand
something of the politics of ancient Greece and Rome.

There have been many controversial aspects to the 2008
presidential election, but one thing is uncontroversial:
that Obama's skill as an orator has been one of the
most important factors – perhaps the most important
factor – in his victory. The sheer numbers of people
who have heard him speak live set him apart from his
rivals – and, indeed, recall the politics of ancient
Athens, where the public speech given to ordinary
voters was the motor of politics, and where the art of
rhetoric matured alongside democracy.

Obama has bucked the trend of recent presidents – not
excluding Bill Clinton – for dumbing down speeches.
Elvin T. Lim's book The Anti-Intellectual Presidency: The
Decline of Presidential Rhetoric from George Washington to
George W. Bush, submits presidential oratory to
statistical analysis. He concludes that 100 years ago
speeches were pitched at college reading level. Now they
are at eighth grade. Obama's speeches, by contrast, flatter
their audience. His best speeches are adroit literary
creations, rich, like those Doric columns, with allusion,
his turn of phrase consciously evoking lines by Lincoln

and King, by Woody Guthrie and Sam Cooke. Though
he has speechwriters, he does much of the work himself.
(Jon Favreau, the 27-year-old who heads Obama's
speechwriting team, has said that his job is like being
'Ted Williams's batting coach'.) James Wood, professor
of the practice of literary criticism at Harvard, has
already performed a close-reading exercise on the
victory speech for the New Yorker. Can you imagine the
same being done of a George W. Bush speech?

More than once, the adjective that has been deployed to
describe Obama's oratorical skill is 'Ciceronian'. Cicero,
the outstanding Roman politician of the late republic,
was certainly the greatest orator of his time, and one of
the greatest in history. A fierce defender of the
republican constitution, his criticism of Mark Antony
got him murdered in 43 BC.

During the Roman republic (and in ancient Athens)
politics was oratory. In Athens, questions such as
whether or not to declare war on an enemy state were
decided by the entire electorate (or however many
bothered to turn up) in open debate. Oratory was the
supreme political skill, on whose mastery power
depended. Unsurprisingly, then, oratory was highly
organized and rigorously analyzed. The Greeks and
Romans, in short, knew all the rhetorical tricks, and
they put a name to most of them.

It turns out that Obama knows them, too. One of the
best known of Cicero's techniques is his use of series of
three to emphasize points: the tricolon. (The most
enduring example of a Latin tricolon is not Cicero's,

but Caesar's *Veni, vidi, vici* – 'I came, I saw, I conquered'.)
Obama uses tricola freely. Here's an example: 'Tonight,
we gather to affirm the greatness of our nation, not
because of the height of our skyscrapers, or the power
of our military, or the size of our economy…'. In this
passage, from the 2004 Democratic convention speech,
Obama is also using the technique of 'praeteritio' –
drawing attention to a subject by not discussing it.
(He is discounting the height of America's skyscrapers
etc, but in so doing reminds us of their importance.)

One of my favourites among Obama's tricks was his use
of the phrase 'a young preacher from Georgia', when
accepting the Democratic nomination in August 2008;
he did not name Martin Luther King. The term for the
technique is 'antonomasia'. One example from Cicero is
the way he refers to Phoenix, Achilles' mentor in the
Iliad, as 'senior magister' – 'the aged teacher'. In both
cases, it sets up an intimacy between speaker and
audience, the flattering idea that we all know what we
are talking about without need for further exposition. It
humanizes the character – King was just an ordinary
young man, once. Referring to Georgia by name
localizes the reference – Obama likes to use the specifics
of American places to ground the winged sweep of his
rhetoric – just as in his 4 November speech: 'Our
campaign… began in the backyards of Des Moines and
the living rooms of Concord and the front porches of
Charleston', which, of course, is also another tricolon.

Obama's favourite tricks of the trade, it appears, are
the related anaphora and epiphora. Anaphora is the
repetition of a phrase at the start of a sentence. Again,

from 4 November: 'It's the answer told by lines that stretched around schools... It's the answer spoken by young and old... It's the answer...'. Epiphora does the same, but at the end of a sentence. From the same speech (yet another tricolon): 'She lives to see them stand out and speak up and reach for the ballot. Yes we can'. The phrase 'Yes we can' completes the next five paragraphs.

That 'Yes we can' refrain might more readily summon up the call-and-response preaching of the American church than classical rhetoric. And, of course, Obama has been influenced by his time in the congregations of powerfully effective preachers. But James Davidson, reader in ancient history at the University of Warwick, points out that preaching itself originates in ancient Greece. 'The tradition of classical oratory was central to the early church, when rhetoric was one of the most important parts of education. Through sermons, the church captured the rhetorical tradition of the ancients. America has preserved that, particularly in the black church.'

It is not just in the intricacies of speechifying that Obama recalls Cicero. Like Cicero, Obama is a lawyer. Like Cicero, Obama is a writer of enormous accomplishment – Dreams From My Father, Obama's first book, will surely enter the American literary canon. Like Cicero, Obama is a novus homo – the Latin phrase means 'new man' in the sense of self-made. Like Cicero, Obama entered politics without family backing (compare Clinton) or a military record (compare John McCain). Roman tradition dictated you had both.

The compensatory talent Obama shares with Cicero, says Catherine Steel, professor of classics at the University of Glasgow, is a skill at 'setting up a genealogy of forebears – not biological forebears but intellectual forebears. For Cicero it was Licinius Crassus, Scipio Aemilianus and Cato the Elder. For Obama it is Lincoln, Roosevelt and King'.

Steel also points out how Obama's oratory conforms to the tripartite ideal laid down by Aristotle, who stated that good rhetoric should consist of *pathos*, *logos* and *ethos* – emotion, argument and character. It is in the projection of *ethos* that Obama particularly excels. Take this resounding passage: 'I am the son of a black man from Kenya and a white woman from Kansas. I was raised with the help of a white grandfather who survived a Depression to serve in Patton's army during World War II and a white grandmother who worked on a bomber assembly line at Fort Leavenworth while he was overseas. I've gone to some of the best schools in America and lived in one of the world's poorest nations.' He manages to convey the sense that not only can he revive the American dream, but that he personally embodies – actually, in some sense, is – the American dream.

In English, when we use the word 'rhetoric', it is generally preceded by the word 'empty'. Rhetoric has a bad reputation. McCain warned lest an electorate be 'deceived by an eloquent but empty call for change'. Waspishly, Clinton noted, 'You campaign in poetry, you govern in prose.' The Athenians, too, knew the dangers of a populace's being swept along by a persuasive but unscrupulous demagogue (and they invented the word). And it was the Roman politician Cato – though it could have been McCain – who said *Rem tene, verba sequentur*. ' If you hold on to the facts, the words will follow.'

Cicero was well aware of the problem. In his book On the Orator, he argues that real eloquence can be acquired only if the speaker has attained the highest state of knowledge – 'otherwise what he says is just an empty and ridiculous swirl of verbiage'. The true orator is one whose practice of citizenship embodies a civic ideal – whose rhetoric, far from empty, is the deliberate, rational, careful organizer of ideas and argument that propels the state forward safely and wisely. This is clearly what Obama, too, is aiming to embody: his project is to unite rhetoric, thought and action in a new politics that eschews narrow bipartisanship. Can Obama's words translate into deeds? The presidency of George Bush provided plenty of evidence that a man who has problems with his prepositions may also struggle to govern well. We can only hope that Obama's presidency proves that opposite.

Charlotte Higgins

Charlotte Higgins is the author of It's All Greek To Me: From Homer to the Hippocratic Oath, How Ancient Greece Has Shaped Our World (Short Books) and is the chief arts writer for the Guardian.

Introduction

OBAMA'S EARLY YEARS (1961–1998)

Born on 4 August 1961 in Honolulu, Hawaii, Barack
Hussein Obama, Jr, came from a most unusual
background for an American of his time. His mother,
Ann Dunham, was a white girl of Anglo-Irish heritage
from Kansas. His father, Barack Hussein Obama, was
a black Kenyan who was studying economics at the
University of Hawaii. They married on 2 February
1961, when Ann – then aged 18 – was three months'
pregnant; Hawaii was one of only 22 US states in
which interracial marriage was then legal.

In 1963, Obama's father left Hawaii alone to continue
his studies at Harvard University; he later returned to
Kenya and saw the young Barack only once more, in
1971. Barack, Sr, was killed in a road accident in 1982.

Meanwhile, Ann was granted a divorce in 1964. Two years later she married again, this time to Lolo Soetoro, a graduate geography student from Indonesia, who then took his wife and stepson to live in Jakarta. There Barack Obama, Jr, attended elementary schools until 1971, when he returned to Honolulu to live with his maternal grandparents, Stanley and Madelyn Dunham. (Stanley, who was also from Kansas and had moved to Hawaii for work, died in 1992; Madelyn lived until 2 November 2008, two days before her grandson was elected president of the United States.)

On completing his high school education, Barack Obama continued his studies on the US mainland, first at Occidental College in Los Angeles and then at Columbia University, New York, from which he graduated in 1983 with a degree in political science. After a series of jobs as a writer and researcher and a visit to Kenya, where he met his late father's family for the first time, he entered Harvard Law School in 1988. A year later, while working during the vacation at the Chicago law firm of Sidley Austin, Obama met Michelle Robinson, a young lawyer at the same partnership.

In 1991, Obama graduated magna cum laude from Harvard Law School, where he was the first African American president of the *Harvard Law Review*. He then worked as a director of Project Vote, an initiative that enrolled 37.5 per cent of the 400,000 African Americans in Illinois who had previously not been on the state's electoral register. In October 1992, he married Michelle and started work as a lecturer in constitutional law at the University of Chicago Law School.

While continuing work as a lecturer, Barack Obama joined Miner, Barnhill & Galland, a Chicago law firm specializing in civil rights litigation and neighbourhood economic development. In his spare time, he wrote *Dreams From My Father*. This memoir – currently the main source of information about his early life and career – is an unusually candid work, one of very few political autobiographies that rise above self-serving and attempt to reveal the subject, warts and all. It is also remarkably literary in style. It was published in August 1995 to what has been described as 'light praise and attention'. Three months later, Obama's mother, Ann Dunham Soetoro, died of ovarian cancer.

In 1996, Barack Obama was elected to the Illinois State Senate as the senator from Hyde Park, the residential suburb of Chicago in which he and Michelle had made their home. In his first term he established a reputation as a formidable debater and an outstanding orator as he worked to pass legislation that tightened campaign finance regulations, expanded health care for poor families, and reformed criminal justice and welfare laws.

In July 1998, Obama became a father for the first time, when his daughter Malia was born (his second daughter, Natasha, was born in 2001); at the end of that year he was reelected to the Illinois Senate for a second term.

Chapter 1

THE ILLINOIS SENATE
(1998–2005)

In October 2002, Barack Obama made a speech against the US invasion of Iraq that brought the rising Hawaiian-born politician to the attention of an audience beyond his adopted state. In July 2004, Obama wrote and delivered the keynote address at the Democratic National Convention; in January 2005 he became a US senator from Illinois, only the third African American to sit in the Upper House since 1877.

In his first year in Congress he made memorable speeches on a range of subjects, from civil rights (pages 26 and 34) to the challenges faced by single parents (page 35), and thereby announced himself as a politician with vision and the oratorical skill to communicate it. He also coined a phrase to describe one of the phenomena that he most vigorously opposed, 'the timidity of politics' (page 38).

Stance on the War on Terror

2 October 2002, Federal Plaza, Chicago, Illinois

In October 2002, Barack Obama – by this time an established state senator – gave a public address in Chicago in which he staked out his position on the War on Terror – the invasion by the United States and its allies of Afghanistan and Iraq in pursuit of Al Qaeda, the terrorist organization responsible for the destruction of the World Trade Center and other attacks on the United States on 11 September 2001. In the course of this speech, he repeats the crucial ideas over and over again. One message is that he is not a peacenik: he is not against armed conflict in principle.

Obama states that he is 'not opposed to war' a total of five times and uses the verb 'opposed' a further seven times in other forms to make it clear what he is against, namely 'a dumb war', a phrase he uses three times. He also begins four sections of the speech with the rhetorical question, 'You want a fight, President Bush?' (George W. Bush, President of the United States, 2001–9), before adducing reasons why this is the wrong fight, at the wrong time, against the wrong enemy.

... I suffer no illusions about Saddam Hussein [president of Iraq, 1979–2003]. He is a brutal man. A ruthless man. A man who butchers his own people to secure his own power. He has repeatedly defied UN resolutions, thwarted UN inspection teams, developed chemical and biological weapons, and coveted nuclear capacity. He's a bad guy. The world, and the Iraqi people, would be better off without him...

... I also know that Saddam poses no imminent and direct threat to the United States, or to his neighbours, that the Iraqi economy is in shambles, that the Iraqi military is a fraction of its former strength, and that in concert with the international community he can be contained until, in the way of all petty dictators, he falls away into the dustbin of history...

I am not opposed to all wars. I'm opposed to dumb wars. So for those of us who seek a more just and secure world for our children, let us send a clear message to the President.

You want a fight, President Bush? Let's finish the fight with Bin Laden and Al Qaeda, through effective, coordinated intelligence, and a shutting down of the financial networks that support terrorism...

You want a fight, President Bush? Let's fight to make sure that the UN inspectors can do their work, and that we vigorously enforce a non-proliferation treaty, and that former enemies and current allies like Russia safeguard and ultimately eliminate their stores of nuclear material, and that nations like Pakistan and India never use the terrible weapons already in their possession, and that the arms merchants in our own country stop feeding the countless wars that rage across the globe.

You want a fight, President Bush? Let's fight to make sure our so-called allies in the Middle East, the Saudis and the Egyptians, stop oppressing their own people, and suppressing dissent, and tolerating corruption and inequality, and mismanaging their economies so that their youth grow up without education, without prospects, without hope, the ready recruits of terrorist cells.

You want a fight, President Bush? Let's fight to wean ourselves off Middle East oil through an energy policy that doesn't simply serve the interests of Exxon and Mobil.

Those are the battles that we need to fight. Those are the battles that we willingly join. The battles against ignorance and intolerance. Corruption and greed. Poverty and despair.

The consequences of war are dire, the sacrifices immeasurable. We may have occasion in our lifetime to once again rise up in defence of our freedom and pay the wages of war. But we ought not – we will not – travel down that hellish path blindly. Nor should we allow those who would march off and pay the ultimate sacrifice, who would prove the full measure of devotion with their blood, to make such an awful sacrifice in vain.

Keynote Address, Democratic National Convention

27 July 2004, Boston, Massachusetts

On 27 July 2004, Barack Obama gave the keynote address at the Democratic National Convention in support of John Kerry, the party's presidential candidate in that year's forthcoming election. This is widely regarded as the speech in which the US senator from Illinois extended his appeal beyond party activists by using an account of his own life to establish the idea that all Americans are connected in ways that transcend political, cultural and geographical differences. He later expanded some of his ideas into a full-length book, *The Audacity of Hope*.

The speech features several of the rhetorical devices identified in Charlotte Higgins's Foreword. Obama's powers of rhetoric are such that he can make criticisms of the Republican administration without hitting a false note. As a politician, he makes his point, but he avoids making it sound like point-scoring – the reference in the sixth paragraph to uncounted votes harks back to the 2000 US presidential election, in which the Republican George W. Bush beat the Democrat Al Gore only after a bitter dispute about the conduct of the electoral process in Florida.

... Tonight is a particular honour for me because, let's face it, my presence on this stage is pretty unlikely. My father was a foreign student, born and raised in a small village in Kenya. He grew up herding goats, went to school in a tin-roof shack. His father, my grandfather, was a cook, a domestic servant.

But my grandfather had larger dreams for his son. Through hard work and perseverance my father got a scholarship to study in a magical place: America, which stood as a beacon of freedom and opportunity to so many who had come before. While studying here, my father met my mother. She was born in a town on the other side of the world, in Kansas. Her father worked on oil rigs and farms through most of the Depression [worldwide economic downturn, 1929–39]. The day after Pearl Harbor [7 December 1941 Japanese air attack on US naval dockyard in Hawaii that brought the United States into the Second World War] he signed up for duty, joined [General George S.] Patton's army and marched across Europe. Back home, my grandmother raised their baby and went to work on a bomber assembly line. After the war, they studied on the GI Bill, bought a house through FHA [the Federal Housing Administration, a part of the New Deal of President Franklin D. Roosevelt, 1933–1945], and moved west in search of opportunity.

And they, too, had big dreams for their daughter, a common dream, born of two continents. My parents shared not only an improbable love; they shared an abiding faith in the possibilities of this nation. They would give me an African name, Barack, or 'blessed', believing that in a tolerant America your name is no barrier to success. They imagined me going to the best schools in the land, even though they weren't rich, because in a generous America you don't have to be rich to achieve your potential. They are both passed away now. Yet, I know that, on this night, they look down on me with pride.

I stand here today, grateful for the diversity of my heritage, aware that my parents' dreams live on in my precious daughters. I stand here knowing that my story is part of the larger American story, that I owe a debt to all of those who came before me, and that, in no other country on earth, is my story even possible.

Tonight, we gather to affirm the greatness of our nation, not because of the height of our skyscrapers, or the power of our military, or the size of our economy...

... That is the true genius of America, a faith in the simple dreams of its people, the insistence on small miracles. That we can tuck in our children at night and know they are fed and clothed and safe from harm. That we can say what we think, write what we think, without hearing a sudden knock on the door. That we can have an idea and start our own business without paying a bribe or hiring somebody's son. That we can participate in the political process without fear of retribution, and that our votes will be counted – or at least, most of the time...

... I say to them tonight, there's not a liberal America and a conservative America – there's the United States of America. There's not a black America and white America and Latino America and Asian America; there's the United States of America. The pundits like to slice-and-dice our country into Red States and Blue States; Red States for Republicans, Blue States for Democrats. But I've got news for them, too. We worship an awesome God in the Blue States, and we don't like federal agents poking around our libraries in the Red States. We coach Little League [a non-profit organization that runs baseball and softball matches for under-13s; enshrined in the United States code as one of the nation's Patriotic Societies and Observances, and thus strongly associated with Republicanism] in the Blue States and have gay friends in the Red States. There are patriots who opposed the war in Iraq and patriots who supported it. We are one people, all of us pledging allegiance to the stars and stripes, all of us defending the United States of America...

Birthday Tribute to a Civil Rights Hero

21 February 2005, Atlanta, Georgia

John Lewis (b. 1940) is an African American who took part in the Freedom Rides, a series of political protests by blacks and whites who in 1961 travelled together on buses in the American South in defiance of racial segregation laws. In March 1965, he was among a group of protesters attacked by state troopers as they tried to cross a bridge in Selma, Alabama. Lewis suffered severe wounds, the scars of which are still visible on his head. In 1986 he was elected to the US Congress as a representative of Georgia's Fifth District. On 21 February 2005 – Lewis's 65th birthday – Barack Obama spoke at a gala dinner.

The phrase 'audacity of hope' is thought to have been inspired by his pastor, Jeremiah Wright (see page 105), who based a 1990 sermon on 'Hope', a painting by British artist George Frederic Watts (1817–1904) of a woman sitting on top of the world playing a harp. The simile 'as timeless as our hopes' reinforces the notion that Americans down the ages have shared the same values and helps to establish that civil rights, for so long a controversial topic, are now regarded as common ground. Note also the four rhetorical questions and the effective opening of 13 sentences with the word 'and'.

I've often thought about the people on the Edmund Pettus Bridge that day. Not only John and [US civil rights campaigner] Hosea Williams leading the march, but the hundreds of everyday Americans who left their homes and their churches to join it. Blacks and whites, teenagers and children, teachers and bankers and shopkeepers – a beloved community of God's children ready to stand for freedom.

And I wonder, where did they find that kind of courage? When you're facing row after row of state troopers on horseback armed with billy clubs and tear gas, when they're coming toward you spewing hatred and violence, how do you simply stop, kneel down, and pray to the Lord for salvation? Truly, this is the audacity of hope.

But the most amazing thing of all is that after that day – after John Lewis was beaten within an inch of his life, after people's heads were gashed open and their eyes were burned and they watched their children's innocence literally beaten out of them – after all that, they went back to march again.

They marched again. They crossed the bridge. They awakened a nation's conscience, and not five months later, the Voting Rights Act of 1965 was signed into law.

And so it was, in a story as old as our beginnings and as timeless as our hopes, that change came about because the good people of a great nation willed it so.

Thank you, John, for going back. Thank you for marching again.

Thank you for reminding us that in America, ordinary citizens can somehow find in their hearts the courage to do extraordinary things. That in the face of the fiercest resistance and the most crushing oppression, one voice can be willing to stand up and say that's wrong and this is right and here's why. And say it again. And say it louder. And keep saying it until other voices join the chorus to sing the songs that set us free.

Today, I'm sure you'll all agree that we have songs left to sing and bridges left to cross. And if there's anything we can learn from this living saint sitting beside me, it is that change is never easy, but always possible. That it comes not from violence or militancy or the kind of politics that pits us against each other and plays on our worst fears; but from great discipline and organization, from a strong message of hope, and from the courage to turn against the tide so that the tide eventually may be turned.

Today, we need that courage. We need the courage to say that it's wrong that one out of every five children is born into poverty in the richest country on Earth. And it's right to do whatever necessary to provide our children the care and the education they need to live up to their God-given potential.

It's wrong to tell hardworking families who are earning less and paying more in taxes that we can't do anything to help them buy their own home or send their kids to college or care for them when they're sick. And it's right to expect that if you're willing to work hard in this country of American Dreamers, the sky is the limit on what you can achieve.

It's wrong to tell those brave men and women who are willing to fight and die for this country that when they come home, we may not have room for them at the VA hospitals or the benefits we promised them. And it's right to always provide the very best care for the very best of America.

My friends, we have not come this far as a people and a nation because we believe that we're better off simply fending for ourselves. We are here because we believe that all men are created equal, and that we are all connected to each other as one people. And we need to say that more. And say it again. And keep saying it. And where will our courage come from to speak these truths? When we stand on our own Edmund Pettus Bridge, what hope will sustain us?

I believe it is the hope of knowing that people like John Lewis have stood on that same bridge and lived to cross it.

Transcending the Party Divide Speech

13 April 2005, US Senate, Washington, D.C.

On 13 April 2005, just over three months after taking his seat in the US Congress as the junior senator from Illinois, Barack Obama demonstrated for the first time in the Upper House that he was not going to be a low partisan politician, but that he would aim for the broad, sweeping view of the statesman and try to bring the concerns of Americans outside the Capitol to the attention of the Senate. Such sentiments are easy to

spout – they are the small change of populist oratory –
but what raises Obama's speech above the ordinary is,
as so often, his use of language, particularly the phrase
'disagree without being disagreeable'.

... I urge you to think not just about winning every
debate, but about protecting free and democratic debate.
During my Senate campaign, I had the privilege and
the opportunity to meet Americans from all walks of
life and both ends of the political spectrum. They told
me about their lives, about their hopes, about the issues
that mattered to them, and they also told me what they
think about Washington.

Because you've all heard it yourselves, I know it won't
surprise many of you to learn that a lot of people don't
think much gets done around here about the issues
they care most about. They think the atmosphere has
become too partisan, the arguments have become too
nasty, and the political agendas have become too petty.

And while I haven't been here too long, I've noticed
that partisan debate is sharp, and dissent is not always
well-received. Honest differences of opinion and
principled compromise often seem to be the victim of a
determination to score points against one's opponents.

But the American people sent us here to be their voice.
They understand that those voices can at times become
loud and argumentative, but they also hope that we can
disagree without being disagreeable. And at the end of
the day, they expect both parties to work together to get
the people's business done.

'Our Past, Our Future, Our Vision': Thoughts on Lincoln
20 April 2005, Abraham Lincoln
Presidential Library and Museum,
Washington, D.C.

On 20 April 2005, Barack Obama made the following speech at the Abraham Lincoln Presidential Library and Museum. As would be expected of any politician in such a setting, he made much of the great president (1861–5) after whom the foundation is named. What might have sounded like mere lip service is here elevated by Obama's acknowledgement of Lincoln's flawed humanity.

... what separates Lincoln from the other great men has to do with something else. It's an issue of character that speaks to us, of moral resolve. Lincoln was not a perfect man, nor a perfect president. By modern standards, his condemnation of slavery might be considered tentative; his Emancipation Proclamation [executive orders in 1862 and 1863 that freed all US slaves] more a military document than a clarion call for justice. He wasn't immune to political considerations; his temperament could be indecisive and morose.

And yet despite these imperfections, despite his fallibility – indeed, perhaps because of a painful self-awareness of his own failings, etched in every crease of his face and reflected in those haunted eyes – because of this essential humanity of his, when it came time to confront the greatest moral challenge this nation has ever faced, Lincoln did not flinch.

He did not equivocate or duck or pass the challenge on to future generations. He did not demonize the fathers and sons who did battle on the other side, nor seek to diminish the terrible costs of his war [the American Civil War, 1861–5]. In the midst of slavery's dark storm and the complexities of governing a house divided, he kept his moral compass pointed firm and true.

Hurricane Katrina, Speech,

6 September 2005, Houston, Texas

On 29 August 2005, New Orleans was devastated by Hurricane Katrina. Among the first politicians to survey the damage was Barack Obama. In this speech, Obama again stresses his statesmanship: he cares nothing for race, class or political affiliation; he is concerned only about the city's social problems and the human tragedy.

... I hope that out of this crisis we all begin to reflect – Democrat and Republican – on not only our individual responsibilities to ourselves and our families, but to our mutual responsibilities to our fellow Americans. I hope we realise that the people of New Orleans weren't just abandoned during the Hurricane. They were abandoned long ago – to murder and mayhem in their streets; to substandard schools; to dilapidated housing; to inadequate health care; to a pervasive sense of hopelessness.

That is the deeper shame of this past week – that it has taken a crisis like this one to awaken us to the great divide that continues to fester in our midst. That's what all Americans are truly ashamed about, and the fact that we're ashamed about it is a good sign. The fact that all of us – black, white, rich, poor, Republican, Democrat – don't like to see such a reflection of this country we love, tells me that the American people have better instincts and a broader heart than our current politics would indicate.

Rosa Parks's Contribution to America

25 October 2005, US Senate, Washington, D.C.

On 24 October 2005, Rosa Parks died aged 94. Parks was an African American whose refusal, in 1955, to give up her seat to a white passenger led to the Montgomery, Alabama, bus boycott in the segregated American South.

… As we honour the life of Rosa Parks, we should not limit our commemorations to lofty eulogies. Instead, let us commit ourselves to carrying on her fight, one solitary act at a time, and ensure that her passion continues to inspire as it did a half-century ago. That, in my view, is how we can best thank her for her immense contributions to our country.

Rosa Parks once said: 'As long as there is unemployment, war, crime and all things that go to the infliction of man's inhumanity to man, regardless – there is much to be done, and people need to work together.' Now that she's passed, it's up to us to make sure that her message is shared. While we will miss her cherished spirit, let's work to ensure that her legacy lives on in the heart of the nation.

As a personal note, I think it is fair to say were it not for that quiet moment of courage by Mrs Parks, I would not be standing here today. I owe her a great thanks, as does the Nation. She will be sorely missed.

Women's Rights, National Women's Law Center (NWLC)

10 November 2005, Washington, D.C.

In November 2005, Barack Obama outlined his commitment to equality of opportunity for everyone while stressing his credentials as an outsider – someone with no links to what he calls 'Washington'. The main topic of his speech is lone parents but he uses the theme to digress briefly but tellingly into a disquisition on the flaws in the conservative belief in 'trickle-down' – the notion that the state does not need to provide welfare to the needy; all it has to do is minimize taxation.

... for the single mom who's already making less than her male counterpart – the mom who had to go without a paycheque for three months when her daughter was born, who's now facing skyrocketing child care costs and an employer who doesn't provide health care coverage for part-time work – for this mom, getting a few hundred bucks off the next tax bill won't solve the problem, will it?

In Washington, they call this the Ownership Society. But in our past there has been another term for it – Social Darwinism [named after Charles Darwin (1809–82), the British naturalist who formulated the theory of natural selection], every man and woman for him- or herself. It allows us to say to those whose health care or tuition may rise faster than they can afford – tough luck. It allows us to say to the women who lose their jobs when they have to care for a sick child – life isn't fair. It lets us say to the child born into poverty – pull yourself up by your bootstraps.

But there is a problem. It won't work. It ignores our history. Our economic dominance has depended on individual initiative and belief in the free market; but it has also depended on our sense of mutual regard for each other, the idea that everybody has a stake in the country, that we're all in it together and everybody's got a shot at opportunity.

And so if we're serious about this opportunity, if we truly value families and don't think it's right to penalize parenting, then we need to start acting like it. We need to update the social contract in this country to include the realities faced by working women.

When a parent takes parental leave, we shouldn't act like caring for a newborn baby is a three-month break – we should let them keep their salary. When parents are working and their children need care, we should make sure that care is affordable, and we should make sure our kids can go to school earlier and longer so they have a safe place to learn while their parents are at work. When a mom or a dad has to leave work to care for a sick child, we should make sure it doesn't result in a pink slip. When a woman does lose a job, she should get unemployment insurance even if the job loss was due to a family emergency and even if she's looking for a part-time job. And in an economy where health and pension coverage are shrinking, where people switch jobs multiple times and women don't always depend on their husbands for benefits, we should have portable health care plans and pensions that any individual can take with them to any part-time or full-time job and Medicaid that's there when you need it.

... The other day, I was reading through Jonathan Kozol's [b. 1936; US political activist and educational theorist] new book, *Shame of a Nation*, which tells of his travels to underprivileged schools across America.

At one point, Kozol tells about his trip to Fremont High School in Los Angeles, where he met a girl who tells him that she'd taken hairdressing twice, because there were actually two different levels offered by the high school. The first was in hairstyling; the other in braiding.

Another girl, Mireya, listened as her friend told this story. And she began to cry. When asked what was wrong, she said, 'I don't want to take hairdressing. I did not need sewing either. I knew how to sew. My mother is a seamstress in a factory. I'm trying to go to college. I don't need to sew to go to college. My mother sews. I hoped for something else.'

I hoped for something else.

From the first moment a woman dared to speak that hope – dared to believe that the American Dream was meant for her too – ordinary women have taken on extraordinary odds to give their daughters the chance for something else; for a life more equal, more free, and filled with more opportunity than they ever had. In so many ways we have succeeded, but in so many areas we have much work left to do.

Robert F. Kennedy Human Rights Award Ceremony and Commemoration of Robert F. Kennedy's 80th birthday

16 November 2005, Washington, D.C.

The occasion of this speech was an awards ceremony held on what would have been the 80th birthday of Robert F. Kennedy (1925–68), US Attorney General in the administration of his elder brother, John F. Kennedy (President of the United States, 1961–3), and later US senator from New York who was assassinated while campaigning for the Democratic nomination for the US presidency. The most widely quoted extracts from Obama's speech were 'the politics of can't-do and oh-well' and the swipe at Michael D. Brown, the director of the Federal Emergency Management Agency (FEMA) who had been forced to resign in September 2005 following public outcry over his handling of the devastation wrought by Hurricane Katrina.

… It's the timidity of politics that's holding us back right now – the politics of can't-do and oh-well. An energy crisis that jeopardizes our security and our economy? No magic wand to fix it, we're told. Thousands of jobs vanishing overseas? It's actually healthier for the economy that way. Three days late to the worst natural disaster in American history? Brownie, you're doing a heck of a job [this is what President George W. Bush had said approvingly of Michael D. Brown in September; here Obama turns it derisively on its head].

And of course, if nothing can be done to solve the problems we face, if we have no collective responsibility to look out for one another, then the next logical step is to give everyone one big refund on their government – divvy it up into individual tax breaks, hand 'em out, and encourage everyone to go buy their own health care, their own retirement plan, their own child care, their own schools, their own roads, their own levees...

Robert Kennedy... reminds us that we don't need to wait for a hurricane to know that Third World living conditions in the middle of an American city make us all poorer. We don't need to wait for the 3,000th death of someone else's child in Iraq to make us realize that a war without an exit strategy puts all of our families in jeopardy. We don't have to accept the diminishment of the American Dream in this country now, or ever.

It's time for us to meet the whys of today with the why-nots we often quote but rarely live – to answer 'Why hunger?' and 'Why homeless?', 'Why violence?' and 'Why despair?' with 'Why not good jobs and living wages?', 'Why not better health care and world class schools?', 'Why not a country where we make possible the potential that exists in every human being?'

Chapter 2

THE US SENATE
(2006–2007)

Throughout 2006 and into January 2007, Barack
Obama consolidated his reputation in the US Senate
and with the general public through further wide-
ranging addresses on topics of global importance,
including alternative fuels (page 44) and the celebrated
'Take Back America' speech (page 61). Meanwhile, he
kept sight of domestic and local issues – the economy
and labour (page 68) – and worked hard on new
legislation in areas such as lobbying reform (page 42)
and the aftermath of Hurricane Katrina (page 70).
The last was of particular significance because it
expressed a greater concern for the plight of the
devastated city of New Orleans than seemed to have
been shown by the administration of President
George W. Bush.

Ethics and Lobbying Reform

26 January 2006, National Press Club, Washington, D.C.

In this speech, Barack Obama announces proposed
legislation – the CLEANUP Act – against what he
sees as a 'crisis of corruption' in the US capital. He
makes specific attacks on Jack Abramoff, the lobbyist
who on 3 January 2006 had been sentenced to
four years' imprisonment for defrauding Native
Americans of millions of dollars and corrupting
public officials.

… The American people are tired of a Washington
that's only open to those with the most cash and the
right connections. They're tired of a political process
where the vote you cast isn't as important as the favours
you can do. And they're tired of trusting us with their
tax dollars when they see them spent on frivolous pet
projects and corporate giveaways.

It's not that the games that are played in this town are
new or surprising to the public. People are not naïve
to the existence of corruption and they know it has
worn the face of both Republicans and Democrats
over the years…

Now, there's an argument made that somehow this is a
bipartisan scandal. And the defence here is that
everybody does it. Well, not everybody does it. And
people shouldn't lump together those of us who have
to raise funds to run campaigns but do so in a legal
and ethical way with those who invite lobbyists in to
write bad legislation. Those aren't equivalent, and we're
not being partisan by pointing that out…

What's truly offensive about these scandals is that they don't just lead to morally offensive conduct on the part of politicians; they lead to morally offensive legislation that hurts hard-working Americans.

Because when big oil companies are invited into the White House for secret energy meetings, it's no wonder they end up with billions in tax breaks while Americans still struggle to fill up their gas tanks and heat their homes...

When the people running Washington are accountable only to the special interests that fund their campaigns, of course they'll spend your tax dollars with reckless abandon; of course they'll load up bills with pet projects and drive us into deficit with the hope that no one will notice...

The well-connected CEOs and hired guns on K Street [a major thoroughfare in Washington, D.C., in which are located the offices of many special interest groups] who've helped write our laws have gotten what they paid for. They got all the tax breaks and loopholes and access they could ever want. But outside this city, the people who can't afford the high-priced lobbyists and don't want to break the law are wondering, 'When is it our turn? When will someone in Washington stand up for me?'

We need to answer that call because let's face it – for the last few years, the people running Washington simply haven't. And while only some are to blame for the corruption that has plagued this city, all are responsible for fixing it...

Real reform must include real oversight and accountability. Our bill sets up an independent Office of Public Integrity to keep an eye on lobbyists and to make sure they comply with the rules...

Even if we pass a good bill and rid Washington of the Jack Abramoffs of the world, it's going to take much more than gift bans and lobbying reform to restore the public's faith in a government. It will take not simply a change in laws, but a change in attitudes.

Oil and Alternative Fuels: Governor's Ethanol Coalition
28 February 2006, Washington, D.C.

Here Barack Obama sets out details of his proposals for the development of alternative energy sources to reduce US dependence on oil. Before he gets down to the substance, however, he makes a light-hearted stab at the now beleaguered administration of George W. Bush.

... In this year's State of the Union address, President Bush told us that it was time to get serious about America's addiction to foreign oil. The next day, we found out that his idea didn't sit too well with the Saudi royal family. A few hours later, Energy Secretary [Samuel W.] Bodman backtracked and assured the world that even though the President said he planned to reduce the amount of oil we import from the Middle East, he actually didn't mean that literally. If there's a single example out there that encapsulates the ability of unstable, undemocratic governments to wield undue influence over America's national security just because of our dependence on oil, this is it.

Meals Amendment to Ethics and Lobbying Reform Bill

8 March 2006, US Senate, Washington. D.C.

In this speech in support of a move to prevent members of Congress from being wined and dined by lobbyists, Barack Obama shows his awareness that there is no such thing as a free lunch. Although his remarks were addressed in the first instance to fellow legislators, they were really intended for the delectation of a much wider audience of ordinary Americans.

... Of all the ethics reforms we take up this week, this should be an easy one. Because I can't think of a single reason in the world why we shouldn't be paying for our own lunches in Washington.

In cities and towns all across America, people pay for their own lunches and their own dinners. People who make far less than we do. People who can't afford their medical bills or their mortgages or their kids' tuition.

You ask them if they think that the people they send to Congress should be able to rack up a $50 meal on a lobbyists' dime. You ask them if they think we should be able to feast on free steak dinners at fancy restaurants while they're working two jobs just to put food on their table.

Now, in no way do I think that any of my colleagues or staffers would exchange votes for meals. But that's not the point. It's not just the meal that's the problem, it's the perception. It's the access that meal gets you.

In the current Washington culture, lobbyists are expected to pick up the tab when they meet with members or staff. It is simply understood by all sides that the best way to get face time with a member or staffer in order to express your ideas on legislation is to buy them a meal.

But you don't see many members eating $50 meals with constituents who are in town to talk about the issues on their mind or with policy experts who are discussing the latest economic theories. Most of these meals are with high-priced lobbyists who are advocating on behalf of a specific interest. The appearance is that they can afford the access, so they get it...

This isn't about preventing us from interacting with lobbyists who have legitimate business to discuss, and it isn't about preventing staff from getting the information they need to help us pass better policy. We can still do all of this if the ban passes, and we can even do it over lunch or dinner.

All we're asking here is to take out your wallet, pull out your credit card, and pay for your own meal. Everyone else in this country does it – we can do it too.

Immigration Reform

3 April 2006, US Senate, Washington D.C.

In this speech to Congress, Barack Obama deals with the perennially thorny question of immigration. Again, he uses his own family history to typify that of millions of Americans. He also goes back to his 'genealogy of forebears' by referring to Franklin D. Roosevelt (President of the United States, 1933–45). The opening of the penultimate paragraph is a reminder of the speaker's literary nature: some politicians, for whom language is merely a means to an end, would no doubt have said 'We should' or 'We must'; Obama, by contrast, is a lover of words for their own sake and by this time was the established author of a best-selling book, Dreams From My Father. By using the fairly antiquated expression 'It behooves us...', he seeks to attract the educated members of his audience without alienating those who are unfamiliar with the phrase because the latter can easily extrapolate its meaning from the context. This long and complex speech is a cornerstone of Obama's political creed.

I know that this debate evokes strong passions on all sides...

But I believe we can work together to pass immigration reform in a way that unites the people in this country, not in a way that divides us by playing on our worst instincts and fears.

Like millions of Americans, the immigrant story is also my story. My father came here from Kenya, and I represent a state where vibrant immigrant communities ranging from Mexican to Polish to Irish enrich our cities and neighbourhoods. So I understand the allure of freedom and opportunity that fuels the dream of a life in the United States. But I also understand the need to fix a broken system...

To begin with, the agencies charged with border security would receive new technology, new facilities, and more people to stop, process, and deport illegal immigrants. But while security might start at our borders, it doesn't end there. Millions of undocumented immigrants live and work here without our knowing their identity or their background. We need to strike a workable bargain with them. They have to acknowledge that breaking our immigration laws was wrong. They must pay a penalty, and abide by all of our laws going forward. They must earn the right to stay over a six-year period, and then they must wait another five years as legal permanent residents before they become citizens...

Replacing the flood of illegals with a regulated stream of legal immigrants who enter the United States after background checks and who are provided labour rights would enhance our security, raise wages, and improve working conditions for all Americans.

But I fully appreciate that we cannot create a new guestworker programme without making it as close to impossible as we can for illegal workers to find employment. We do not need new guestworkers plus future undocumented immigrants. We need guestworkers instead of undocumented immigrants. Toward that end, American employers need to take responsibility. Too often illegal immigrants are lured here with a promise of a job, only to receive unconscionably low wages. In the interest of cheap labour, unscrupulous employers look the other way when employees provide fraudulent US citizenship documents. Some actually call and place orders for undocumented workers because they don't want to pay minimum wages to American workers in surrounding communities. These acts hurt both American workers and immigrants whose sole aim is to work hard and get ahead. That is why we need a simple, foolproof, and mandatory mechanism for all employers to check the legal status of new hires. Such a mechanism is in the Judiciary Committee bill.

And before any guestworker is hired, the job must be made available to Americans at a decent wage with benefits. Employers then need to show that there are no Americans to take these jobs. I am not willing to take it on faith that there are jobs that Americans will not take...

It is important that if we are going to deal with this problem, we deal with it in a practical, commonsense way. If temporary legal status is granted but the policy says these immigrants are never good enough to become Americans, then the policy makes little sense...

As FDR [Franklin D. Roosevelt] reminded the Nation at the 50th anniversary of the dedication of the Statue of Liberty, those who landed at Ellis Island 'were the men and women who had the supreme courage to strike out for themselves, to abandon language and relatives, to start at the bottom without influence, without money, and without knowledge of life in a very young civilization'.

It behooves us to remember that not every single immigrant who came into the United States through Ellis Island had proper documentation. Not every one of our grandparents or great-grandparents would have necessarily qualified for legal immigration. But they came here in search of a dream, in search of hope. Americans understand that, and they are willing to give an opportunity to those who are already here, as long as we get serious about making sure that our borders actually mean something.

Today's immigrants seek to follow in the same tradition of immigration that has built this country. We do ourselves and them a disservice if we do not recognize the contributions of these individuals. And we fail to protect our Nation if we do not regain control over our immigration system immediately.

Women in Politics:
EMILY'S List Annual Luncheon
11 May 2006, Washington, D.C.

EMILY's List is a Democratic Party action committee that advances the political careers of women who are pro-choice (supporters of the right for women to decide for themselves whether or not to continue with a pregnancy). The name is an acronym of 'Early Money Is Like Yeast', the first half of an American proverb that concludes: 'it helps to raise the dough'.

Before a sympathetic audience, Barack Obama makes a long speech that addresses a wide range of policy issues. He recalls an African American named Marguerite Lewis, whom he had met in Chicago in 2004 when she was 105 years old, and reflects on the changes in the United States since her birth in the final year of the 19th century. He then quotes Newt Gingrich (Republican Speaker of the House of Representatives, 1995–8), who said that the Democrats should adopt a two-word election slogan: 'Had enough?' He takes up this phrase and either quotes or adapts it 20 times.

… These are Americans who still believe in an America where anything's possible – they just don't think their leaders do. These are Americans who still dream big dreams – they just sense their leaders have forgotten how…

[Marguerite Lewis] believed that over a span of three centuries, she had seen enough to know that there is no challenge too great, no injustice too crippling, no destiny too far out of reach for America.

She believed that we don't have to settle for equality for some or opportunity for the lucky or freedom for the few.

And she knew that during those moments in history where it looked like we might give up hope or settle for less, there have always been Americans who refused. Who said we're going to keep on dreaming, and we're going to keep on building, and we're going to keep on marching, and we're going to keep on working because that's who we are. Because we've always fought to bring all of our people under the blanket of the American Dream...

It's the timidity – the smallness – of our politics that's holding us back right now. The idea that some problems are just too big to handle, and if you just ignore them, sooner or later, they'll go away...

Well it's time we finally said we notice, and we care, and we're not gonna settle anymore...

I think we've all had enough. Enough of the broken promises. Enough of the failed leadership. Enough of the can't-do, won't-do, won't-even-try style of governance.

Four years after 9/11, I've had enough of being told that we can find the money to give Paris Hilton [American heiress to the Hilton Hotels chain, famous for her celebrity lifestyle] more tax cuts, but we can't find enough to protect our ports or our railroads or our chemical plants or our borders.

I've had enough of the closed-door deals that give billions to the HMOs [health maintenance organizations] when we're told that we can't do a thing for the 45 million uninsured or the millions more who can't pay their medical bills.

I've had enough of being told that we can't afford body armour for our troops and health care for our veterans. I've had enough of that.

I've had enough of giving billions away to the oil companies when we're told that we can't invest in the renewable energy that will create jobs and lower gas prices and finally free us from our dependence on the oil wells of Saudi Arabia.

I've had enough of our kids going to schools where the rats outnumber the computers. I've had enough of [Hurricane] Katrina survivors living out of their cars and begging FEMA [Federal Emergency Management Agency] for trailers. And I've had enough of being told that all we can do about this is sit and wait and hope that the good fortune of a few trickles on down to everyone else in this country...

So yes, I've had enough. And if you've had enough too, then we got some work to do. If you've had enough, then we have some cheques to write, and some calls to make, and some doors to knock on...

Health Care and Health Issues: Commencement Address

20 May 2006, Southern Illinois University School of Medicine, Springfield, Illinois

Congratulating a class of young doctors who are about to take up their residencies – 'commencement' is the US equivalent of the British 'graduation' – Barack Obama makes some wider points about health care provisions in the United States. Note at the end of the first paragraph how he flips from 'you' to 'we' – this may be a slip, but it is more likely to be deliberate inclusiveness. Certainly, inclusiveness is evident later in the speech where, although Obama is plainly confident that he is preaching to the mainly converted, he acknowledges that no one has to share his views about public service – an approach that forestalls any suggestion that he is merely a politician making his political points, regardless of the audience.

... Life often happens in a way that makes it easy for us to miss the larger obligations we have toward one another. The demands of work and time and money tend to narrow our focus and cause us to turn inward. You might flip on the news or pick up the paper and feel moved by a story about genocide in Darfur [war-torn province of Sudan] or the AIDS epidemic or the 15-year-old who was gunned down in front of his house. You may even feel compelled to do something about it. But inevitably, it becomes time to study, or go to work, or cook dinner, or put the kids to bed – and so we often turn away from the big stuff and concentrate on simply surviving the small.

This is perfectly human. It is perfectly understandable. And yet, the survival of our country has always required more. It has required ordinary men and women to look beyond their own lives; to think about the larger challenges we face as a people – and then rise to meet them.

This is what I'd like to ask you to do today...

At some point in your residency, you'll see firsthand that there is something fundamentally broken about our health care system. You'll realize that for millions upon millions of Americans, the care you provide is becoming far too costly for them to afford. And you'll have to decide what, if anything, you're going to do about it…

It's a cost crisis that traps us all in a vicious cycle. Because the uninsured can't afford health care, they put off seeing a doctor or end up in the ER [A&E] when they get sick. Then their care is more expensive, and so premiums for all Americans go up. Because everyone's premiums go up, more Americans lose their health care…

And so today I ask you to be more than just practitioners of medicine; I ask you to be advocates for medicine. I ask you to be advocates for a health care system that is fair, that is just, and that provides every single American with the best your profession has to offer.

Just like generations before, you must dare to believe… You must choose: will the medical miracles you perform over the next generation reach only the luckiest few? Or will history look back at this moment as the time when we finally made care available at a cost that we can afford?

There isn't one person sitting here today who wants to turn a sick patient away because they can't pay. Not one person who wants the care they deliver denied to those whose lives depend on it. Each of you has dedicated yourselves to this calling because where there is a sick person, you want to heal them. Where there is a life in jeopardy, you want to save it.

And so today, when you leave here, it will not only be with great knowledge, but with even greater responsibility.

Because if we do nothing about the rising cost of health care, it will keep climbing, and in ten years, the number of uninsured could grow to 54 million...

We need you to dream, we need you to speak out, and we need you to act. And together, we can build a health care system in this country that finally works for every American...

... no one's forcing you to care.

But I hope that you do...

When you think about these challenges, I also ask you to remember that in this country, our history of overcoming the seemingly impossible always comes about because individuals who care really can make a difference...

And as you go forth from here in your own life, you can keep this history alive if you only find the courage to try.

University of Massachusetts at Boston Commencement Address
2 June 2006, Boston, Massachusetts

In this speech to a year of newly graduated students, Obama encourages the audience to follow their dreams, as he and his father had done. Note the ways in which he refers to Abraham Lincoln and Martin Luther King, Jr (African American clergyman and civil rights leader 1929–68) without naming them – the former he calls 'a young man from Illinois', the latter 'a young black minister from Georgia'.

... It's your turn to keep this daringly radical but unfailingly simple notion of America alive – that no matter where you're born or how much your parents have; no matter what you look like or what you believe in, you can still rise to become whatever you want; still go on to achieve great things; still pursue the happiness you hope for.

Today, this dream sounds common – perhaps even cliché – yet for most of human history it's been anything but. As a servant of Rome, a peasant in China, or a subject of King George [King George III of Great Britain, ruled 1760–1820; during his reign, the United States won independence] there were very few unlikely futures. No matter how hard you worked or struggled for something better, you knew you'd spend your life forced to build somebody else's empire; to sacrifice for someone else's cause.

But as the centuries passed, the people of the world grew restless. They were tired of tyranny and weary of their lot in life.

None of this progress happened on its own. Much of it seemed impossible at the time. But all of it came about because ordinary men and women had faith that here in America, our imperfect dream could be perfected...

I ask you to remember all the amazing and unlikely things that have happened in this country. This country

where a young man from Illinois who failed at so many
of the business and political ventures he attempted still
went on to become the president who freed a people
and saved a union. This country where a young black
minister from Georgia who had nothing but a dream in
his heart went on to lead his people to the promised
land of civil rights and voting rights. This country
where hundreds of parents all over the world who never
had the chance to further their education could still
watch their children become the first in their family to
earn a degree on a hopeful Boston day in June.

This is America. A place where millions of restless
adventurers from all over the world, still weary of their
lot in life – still hoping for something better – have
longed to travel great distances and take great risks for
a chance to arrive on our shores.

My father was one of them. Born and raised in Kenya
before that nation was freed from the shackles of
colonialism, he grew up herding his father's goats and,
from time to time, attending local schools.

But he wanted more. He dreamed of coming to
America so he could further his education, improve his
skills, and then return to help lead the next generation
of newly independent Kenyans.

You will be tested. You won't always succeed. But know
that you have it within your power to try. That
generations who have come before you faced these
same fears and uncertainties in their own time. And
that through our collective labour, and through God's

providence, and our willingness to shoulder each other's burdens, America will continue on its journey towards that distant horizon, and a better day.

'Our Past, Our Future and Vision for America': Take Back America Conference
14 June, 2006, Washington, D.C.

This landmark address has become known as the 'Take Back America' speech even though Barack Obama does not use these words anywhere in it. Much of the material he had used previously – the story of Marguerite Lewis (page 52), the passage about 'the timidity – the smallness – of our politics' (page 38) and Newt Gingrich's 'Had enough?' (page 52) – but here it is synthesized into a greater whole.

… My friends, we meet here today at a time where we find ourselves at a crossroads in America's history… You hear people say that we've finally arrived at a moment where something must change.

These are Americans who still believe in an America where anything's possible – they just don't think their leaders do. These are Americans who still dream big dreams – they just sense their leaders have forgotten how…

In a century just six years old, our faith has been shaken by war and terror, disaster and despair, threats to the middle-class dream, and scandal and corruption in our government…

But while the world has changed around us, too often our government has stood still. Our faith has been shaken, but the people running Washington aren't willing to make us believe again.

Well it's time we finally said we notice, and we care, and we're not gonna settle anymore...

We know that government can't solve all our problems – and we don't want it to.

But we also know that there are some things we can't do on our own. We know that there are some things we do better together... That we have individual responsibility, but we also have collective responsibility to each other.

That's what America is...

Ladies and gentlemen, this is our time.

Our time to make a mark on history.

Our time to write a new chapter in the American story.

Our time to leave our children a country that is freer and kinder, more prosperous and more just than the place we grew up.

And then someday, someday, if our kids get the chance to stand where we are and look back at the beginning of the 21st century, they can say that this was the time when America renewed its purpose.

They can say that this was the time when America found its way.

They can say that this was the time when America learned to dream again.

Northwestern University Commencement Address
16 June 2006, Chicago, Illinois

This speech was constructed partly in the form of a response to an article in the Northwestern University student newspaper by Elaine Meyer entitled 'Challenge Us, Senator Obama'. It sets out three lessons that the speaker learned while growing up.

... There's a lot of talk in this country about the federal deficit. But I think we should talk more about our empathy deficit – the ability to put ourselves in someone else's shoes; to see the world through those who are different from us – the child who's hungry, the laid-off steelworker, the immigrant woman cleaning your dorm...

The second lesson I learned after college... Challenge yourself. Take some risks in your life... You can take your diploma, walk off this stage, and go chasing after the big house and the large salary and the nice suits and all the other things that our money culture says you should buy.

But I hope you don't. Focusing your life solely on making a buck shows a poverty of ambition. It asks too little of yourself. And it will leave you unfulfilled...

The third lesson is one that I learned once I got to Chicago... Persevere.

Making your mark on the world is hard. If it were easy, everybody would do it. But it's not. It takes patience, it takes commitment, and it comes with plenty of failure along the way. The real test is not whether you avoid this failure, because you won't. It's whether you let it harden or shame you into inaction, or whether you learn from it; whether you choose to persevere...

What America needs right now, more than ever, is a sense of purpose to guide us through the challenges that lie ahead; a maturity that we seem to have lost somewhere along the way; a willingness to engage in a sober, adult conversation about our future...

Here you sit facing challenges as great as any in the past. And the choice is yours. Will the years pass with barely a whisper from your generation? Or will we look back on this time as the moment where you took a stand and changed the world?

Time will tell. You will be tested by the challenges of this new century, and at times you will fail. But know that you have it within your power to try. That generations who have come before you faced these same fears and uncertainties in their own time. And that if we're willing to shoulder each other's burdens, to take great risks, and to persevere through trial, America will continue on its magnificent journey towards that distant horizon, and a better day.

'Our Past, Our Future and Vision for America': Call to Renewal Keynote Address

28 June 2006, Washington, D.C.

Here Barack Obama describes his own religious beliefs. A long-time worshipper at the Trinity United Church of Christ (a Congregationalist foundation on the South Side of Chicago), he had always held the reservation 'Faith doesn't mean that you don't have doubts.' In this speech Obama asserts an inclusive ecumenism – he wants a United States in which there is room for people of every religion and people of no religion. Many of his points relate to the moral implications of abortion. The balance between the right to life and the right to choose is one of the most divisive questions in contemporary politics. He takes as his starting point the charge by a right-wing Republican that 'Jesus Christ would not vote for Barack Obama because [by being pro-choice, that is, in favour of decisions about abortion being left to those affected] Barack Obama has behaved in a way that it is inconceivable for Christ to have behaved.'

... I answered with what has come to be the typically liberal response in such debates – namely, I said that we live in a pluralistic society, that I can't impose my own religious views on another, that I was running to be the US Senator of Illinois and not the Minister of Illinois...

I think we make a mistake when we fail to acknowledge the power of faith in people's lives – in the lives of the

American people – and I think it's time that we join a serious debate about how to reconcile faith with our modern, pluralistic democracy...

I am not suggesting that every progressive suddenly latch on to religious terminology – that can be dangerous. Nothing is more transparent than inauthentic expressions of faith... some politicians come and clap – off rhythm – to the choir. We don't need that.

In fact, because I do not believe that religious people have a monopoly on morality, I would rather have someone who is grounded in morality and ethics, and who is also secular, affirm their morality and ethics and values without pretending that they're something they're not. They don't need to do that...

But what I am suggesting is this – secularists are wrong when they ask believers to leave their religion at the door before entering into the public square...

So the question is, how do we build on these still-tentative partnerships between religious and secular people of good will? It's going to take more work, a lot more work than we've done so far. The tensions and the suspicions on each side of the religious divide will have to be squarely addressed...

For one, they need to understand the critical role that the separation of church and state has played in preserving not only our democracy, but the robustness of our religious practice.

Moreover, given the increasing diversity of America's population, the dangers of sectarianism have never been greater. Whatever we once were, we are no longer just a Christian nation; we are also a Jewish nation, a Muslim nation, a Buddhist nation, a Hindu nation, and a nation of nonbelievers.

Now this is going to be difficult for some who believe in the inerrancy [the incapability of being wrong] of the Bible, as many evangelicals do. But in a pluralistic democracy, we have no choice. Politics depends on our ability to persuade each other of common aims based on a common reality. It involves the compromise, the art of what's possible. At some fundamental level, religion does not allow for compromise. It's the art of the impossible. If God has spoken, then followers are expected to live up to God's edicts, regardless of the consequences. To base one's life on such uncompromising commitments may be sublime, but to base our policy making on such commitments would be a dangerous thing...

Even those who claim the Bible's inerrancy make distinctions between Scriptural edicts, sensing that some passages – the Ten Commandments, say, or a belief in Christ's divinity – are central to Christian faith, while others are more culturally specific and may be modified to accommodate modern life.

The American people intuitively understand this, which is why the majority of Catholics practice birth control and some of those opposed to gay marriage nevertheless are opposed to a Constitutional amendment to ban it. Religious leadership need not accept such wisdom in counselling their flocks, but they should recognize this wisdom in their politics.

But a sense of proportion should also guide those who police the boundaries between church and state. Not every mention of God in public is a breach to the wall of separation – context matters. It is doubtful that children reciting the Pledge of Allegiance feel oppressed or brainwashed as a consequence of muttering the phrase 'under God'. I certainly didn't.

Economy and Labour

7 August 2006, AFSCME National Convention,
Chicago, Illinois

AFSCME – the American Federation of State, County, and Municipal Employees – is one of the biggest unions in the United States. In this speech, Barack Obama moves fluently from some of the finest moments in the union's history to its present position and future aims. He makes special mention of the strike in 1968 by black sanitation workers of AFSCME Local 1733 in Memphis, Tennessee. They were joined on their protest march by civil rights activist Martin Luther King, Jr, who was shot dead by a sniper on the following day.

… Every year, on April 4th, the sanitation workers of Local 1733 gather again to march the route that led them to justice so long ago.…

They march to remember, but they also march because they know our journey isn't complete – they know we have fights left to win; that we have dreams still unfulfilled.

A few years back, one of these workers, a man named Malcolm Pryor, told a reporter, 'You have to remind people: we are not free yet. As long as I march, Dr King's soul is still rejoicing that people are still trying.'

And so today I ask you to keep marching.

As long as there are those who are jobless, I ask you to keep marching for jobs.

As long as there are those who struggle to raise a family on low wages and few benefits, I ask you to keep marching for opportunity.

As long as there are those who can't organize or unionize or bargain for a better life, I ask you to keep marching for solidarity.

And as long as there are those who try to privatize our government and decimate our social programmes and peddle a philosophy of trickle-down and on-your-own, I ask you to keep marching for a vision of America where we rise or fall as one nation under God.

My friends, it's time again to march for freedom. Time again to march for hope. Time again to march towards the tomorrow that so many have reached for so many times in our past. I know we can get there, and I can't wait to try. Thank you, and good luck.

Katrina and Gulf Recovery: Commencement Address

11 August 2006, Xavier University, New Orleans, Louisiana

Almost a year after Hurricane Katrina, Barack Obama spoke at the graduation ceremony at Xavier University in the still stricken city of New Orleans. He adopted broadly the same approach as at previous commencement (graduation) ceremonies (pages 54, 57 and 63) but he tactfully prefaced his views on empathy with a respectful acknowledgement of the locals' suffering.

...I have to say that I'm pretty humbled to be here. Each year there are hundreds of commencements in this country. All are hopeful, some are inspiring, and most of you probably won't even remember who your speaker was ten years from now. As a rule, they usually involve an old guy like me giving young folks like you advice about what to expect in the real world – advice about the challenges you'll face and the obstacles you'll have to overcome.

But this is different. In the last month, I have walked among New Orleans' battered homes and empty streets and scattered debris that prove armies aren't the only ones who can wage wars on cities. I have seen pictures of Xavier after the storm – the submerged classrooms and the shattered windows and the dorm rooms that were left with books sitting open on desks and clothes still unpacked on the bed...

And as I thought about all of this, it dawned on me that when it comes to giving advice about challenges and obstacles, it's you who could probably teach the rest of us a thing or two about what it takes to overcome.

I could give you a lecture on courage, but some of you know what it is to wait huddled in the dark without electricity or running water, wondering if a helicopter or boat will come for you before the gunshots get closer or the food runs out or the waters rise.

I could talk at length about perseverance, but this is a class that was forced to scatter to schools across the country at the beginning of your senior year, leaving everything you knew behind while you waited to find out if you could ever come back.

And I could go on and on about the importance of community – about what it means to care for each other – but this is a school where so many sacrificed so much in order to open your doors in January; a triumph that showed the rest of America that there are those who refuse to desert this city and its people no matter what...

Some will take an entire lifetime to experience these lessons – others never will. But as some of Katrina's youngest survivors, you've had a front row seat...

And if you remember all of this – if you remember what happened here in New Orleans – if you allow it to change you forever – know that there is another path you can take.

This one is more difficult. It asks more of you. It asks you to leave here and not just pursue your own individual dreams, but to help perfect our collective dream as a nation. It asks you to realize there is more to life than being rich, thin, young, famous, safe, and entertained. It asks you to recognize that there are people out there who need you...

Aside from all the bad that came from Katrina – the failures and the neglect, the incompetence and the apathy – you were also witness to a good that many forgot was even possible.

You saw people from every corner of this country drop what they were doing, leave their homes, and come to New Orleans – Americans who didn't know a soul in the entire city... waded through the streets of this city, saving anyone they could. You saw the doctors and the nurses who refused to leave their city and their patients even when they were told time and again by local officials that it was no longer safe – even when helicopters were waiting to take them away. Men and women who stayed to care for the sick and dying long after their medical equipment and electricity were gone.

And after the storm had passed, you saw a spirit of generosity that spanned an entire globe, with billions upon billions in donations coming from tiny, far-off nations like Qatar and Sri Lanka. Think about that. These are places a lot of folks couldn't even identify on a map. Sri Lanka was still recovering from the devastation caused by last year's Tsunami. And yet, they heard about our tragedy, and they gave.

Remember always this goodness. Remember always that while many in Washington and on all levels of government failed New Orleans, there were plenty of ordinary people who displayed extraordinary humanity during this city's hour of need.

In the years to come, return this favour to those who are forced to weather their own storms – be it the loss of a job or a slide into poverty; an unexpected illness or an unforeseen eviction... Make this a nation where we never again leave behind any American by ensuring that every American has a job that can support a family and health care in case they get sick and a good education for their child and a secure retirement they can count on. Make this a nation where we are never again caught unprepared to meet the challenges of our time...

Make this a nation that is worthy of the sacrifices of so many of its citizens, and in doing so, make real the observation made by a visitor to our country [French political scientist Alexis de Tocqueville, 1805–59] so many centuries ago: 'America is great because Americans are good.'

Chapter 3

THE ROAD TO THE PRESIDENCY

(2006–2007)

In August 2006, Barack Obama entered a new phase of his career during a visit to his father's native Kenya, where he made a remarkable speech that propelled him onto the world stage (page 76). In February 2007, he announced his decision to run for the presidency of the United States (page 87). His chances were thought by many to be restricted by the colour of his skin and by the fact that he had never held high office. He countered these criticisms with the assertion that the very fact that he, an African American, could run for president at all showed the greatness of the modern United States and by turning his acknowledged inexperience into a virtue – he was to be the one serious candidate of either party who was untainted by involvement with previous administrations. The period ends with Obama's rousing 'Turn the Page' speech at the California Democratic National Convention in April 2007 (page 93).

'Our Past, Our Future and Vision for America': an Honest Government, a Hopeful Future

28 August 2006, University of Nairobi, Nairobi, Kenya

This was Barack Obama's second visit to his father's native country; he had previously spent a month there in 1987, on what he described as 'a magical trip' just before he went back to law school in the United States. Returning as a US senator, his Kenyan heritage made it possible for him to counsel his hosts in words that were widely praised as inspirational but which would no doubt have caused bad feeling if they had been uttered by an American with no African links.

… The history of Africa is a history of ancient kingdoms and great traditions; the story of people fighting to be free from colonial rule; the heroism not only of great men like [Kwame] Nkrumah [President of Ghana, 1957–66] and [Jomo] Kenyatta [President of Kenya 1964–78] and [Nelson] Mandela [President of South Africa, 1994–9], but also ordinary people who endured great hardship, from Ghana to South Africa, to secure self-determination in the face of great odds.

But for all the progress that has been made, we must surely acknowledge that neither Kenya nor the African continent have yet fulfilled their potential…

As a Senator from the United States, I believe that my country, and other nations, have an obligation and self-interest in being full partners with Kenya and with Africa. And, I will do my part to shape an intelligent foreign policy that promotes peace and prosperity.

A foreign policy that gives hope and opportunity to the people of this great continent.

But, Kenya must do its part. It cannot wait for other nations to act first. The hard truth is that nations, by and large, will act in their self-interest and if Kenya does not act, it will fall behind...

While corruption is a problem we all share, here in Kenya it is a crisis – a crisis that's robbing an honest people of the opportunities they have fought for – the opportunity they deserve...

In today's Kenya – a Kenya already more open and less repressive than in my father's day – it is that courage that will bring the reform so many of you so desperately want and deserve.

Oil and Alternative Fuels: Energy Independence: A Call for Leadership
20 September 2006, Georgetown University, Washington, D.C.

Here Barack Obama uses two recent news items that have caught his eye – job cuts at the Ford Motor Company and a foiled terrorist attack on oil wells in Yemen – to attack the Bush administration for its failure to develop alternative fuel sources and to outline his own plans for innovation. The third paragraph of this extract contains another example of Obama's fondness for the tricolon device (see Foreword): three sentences begin with 'That's why...'.

... for someone who talks tough about defending America, actually solving our energy crisis seems to factor pretty low on the President's agenda.

And that's because as much as George Bush might want to defend America, he also needs to defend his vision of government – and that's a government that can't, won't, and shouldn't solve great national challenges like our energy dependence.

That's why the President's funding for renewable fuels is at the same level it was the day he took office. That's why his budget funds less than half of the energy bill he himself signed into law. That's why billions of tax dollars that could've been used to fund energy research went to the record-profiting oil companies instead...

With technology we have on the shelves right now and fuels we can grow right here in America, by 2025 we can reduce our oil imports by over 7.5 million barrels per day – an amount greater than all the oil we are expected to import from the entire Middle East...

This is our chance to step up and serve. For decades, we have heard President after President call for energy independence in this country, but for decades, we have fallen short. Well it's time to call on ourselves. We shouldn't wait for the next time gas hits $3 a gallon – and we shouldn't accept any more headlines that talk about a dying auto industry or a terrorist plot to use oil as a weapon against America. We should act – and we should act now.

Now is the time for serious leadership to get us started down the path of energy independence. Now is the time for this call to arms. I hope some of the ideas I've laid out today can serve as a basis for this call, but I also hope that members of both parties and all levels of government can come together in the near future to launch this serious quest for energy independence.

Groundbreaking Ceremony

13 November 2006, Martin Luther King, Jr,
National Memorial, Washington, D.C.

In this tribute to Martin Luther King, Jr, Barack Obama was widely agreed to have achieved something that few politicians before him had ever managed – he honoured the outstanding African American leader of the 1960s' civil rights movement without sounding self-serving, as if trying to associate himself with the great man's memory. Here Obama alludes frequently to King's speeches, notably in the references to Moses (the Old Testament patriarch who led the Children of Israel back to their homeland but did not reach it himself), which recall King's famous line, uttered on 3 April 1968, the day before he was murdered: 'I've seen the promised land. I may not get there with you...' . While making this speech, Obama made no effort to reproduce King's mode of delivery, which many other politicians have attempted but succeeded only in demonstrating the inimitability of the original. Obama looks forward to the time when he brings his children to the memorial:

... At some point, I know that one of my daughters...
perhaps my youngest, will ask, 'Daddy, why is this
monument here? What did this man do?'

How might I answer them? Unlike the others
commemorated in this place, Dr. Martin Luther King,
Jr was not a president of the United States – at no
time in his life did he hold public office. He was not
a hero of foreign wars. He never had much money,
and while he lived he was reviled at least as much as
he was celebrated. By his own accounts, he was a man
frequently racked with doubt, a man not without
flaws, a man who, like Moses before him, more than
once questioned why he had been chosen for so
arduous a task – the task of leading a people to
freedom, the task of healing the festering wounds of
a nation's original sin.

And yet lead a nation he did. Through words he gave
voice to the voiceless. Through deeds he gave courage
to the faint of heart. By dint of vision, and
determination, and most of all faith in the redeeming
power of love, he endured the humiliation of arrest,
the loneliness of a prison cell, the constant threats to
his life, until he finally inspired a nation to transform
itself, and begin to live up to the meaning of its creed.

Like Moses before him, he would never live to see the
Promised Land. But from the mountain top, he
pointed the way for us – a land no longer torn asunder
with racial hatred and ethnic strife, a land that
measured itself by how it treats the least of these, a land
in which strength is defined not simply by the capacity

to wage war but by the determination to forge peace –
a land in which all of God's children might come
together in a spirit of brotherhood...

For all the progress we have made, there are times when
the land of our dreams recedes from us – when we are
lost, wandering spirits, content with our suspicions and
our angers, our long-held grudges and petty disputes,
our frantic diversions and tribal allegiances.

And yet, by erecting this monument, we are reminded
that this different, better place beckons us, and that we
will find it not across distant hills or within some
hidden valley, but rather we will find it somewhere in
our hearts.

A Way Forward in Iraq: Remarks to the Chicago Council on Global Affairs
20 November 2006, Chicago, Illinois

Barack Obama repeats his opposition to the war in Iraq (see page 20) and outlines his plans for the future. While his words did nothing to endear him to the hawks among his compatriots, they were inspiring to those who had agreed from the outset that this campaign was misconceived and founded on false assumptions and bad information. He counsels a more conciliatory foreign policy for the United States.

... Many who supported the original decision to go to
war in Iraq have argued that it has been a failure of
implementation. But I have long believed it has also

been a failure of conception – that the rationale behind the war itself was misguided. And so going forward, I believe there are strategic lessons to be learned from this as we continue to confront the new threats of this new century.

The first is that we should be more modest in our belief that we can impose democracy on a country through military force. In the past, it has been movements for freedom from within tyrannical regimes that have led to flourishing democracies; movements that continue today. This doesn't mean abandoning our values and ideals; wherever we can, it's in our interest to help foster democracy through the diplomatic and economic resources at our disposal. But even as we provide such help, we should be clear that the institutions of democracy – free markets, a free press, a strong civil society – cannot be built overnight, and they cannot be built at the end of a barrel of a gun. And so we must realize that the freedoms FDR [Franklin D. Roosevelt, President of the United States, 1933–45] once spoke of – especially freedom from want and freedom from fear – do not just come from deposing a tyrant and handing out ballots; they are only realized once the personal and material security of a people is ensured as well.

The second lesson is that in any conflict, it is not enough to simply plan for war; you must also plan for success. Much has been written about how the military invasion of Iraq was planned without any thought to what political situation we would find after Baghdad fell. Such lack of foresight is simply inexcusable. If we commit our troops anywhere in the world, it is our solemn responsibility to define their mission and formulate a viable plan to fulfil that mission and bring our troops home.

The final lesson is that in an interconnected world, the defeat of international terrorism – and most importantly, the prevention of these terrorist organizations from obtaining weapons of mass destruction – will require the cooperation of many nations. We must always reserve the right to strike unilaterally at terrorists wherever they may exist. But we should know that our success in doing so is enhanced by engaging our allies so that we receive the crucial diplomatic, military, intelligence, and financial support that can lighten our load and add legitimacy to our actions. This means talking to our friends and, at times, even our enemies...

There have been too many speeches. There have been too many excuses. There have been too many flag-draped coffins, and there have been too many heartbroken families.

The time for waiting in Iraq is over. It is time to change our policy. It is time to give Iraqis their country back. And it is time to refocus America's efforts on the wider struggle yet to be won. Thank you.

The Time Has Come for Universal Health Care: Families USA Conference
25 January 2007, Washington, D.C.

Barack Obama returns to the subject of health care, the government approach to which, he says, typifies 'the smallness of [US] politics'. This speech contains the favourite rhetorical device of repetition of key words – the word 'wrong' occurs five times in quick succession. Note, too, the reference to 'the next president': George W. Bush's term of office still had two years to run, so political commentators were able to read a wider personal significance into the remarks; perhaps Obama was beginning to reveal some of his own plans...

...In the 2008 campaign, affordable, universal health care for every single American must not be a question of whether, it must be a question of how. We have the ideas, we have the resources, and we must find the will to pass a plan by the end of the next president's first term.

I know there's a cynicism out there about whether this can happen, and there's reason for it. Every four years, health care plans are offered up in campaigns with great fanfare and promise. But once those campaigns end, the plans collapse under the weight of Washington politics, leaving the rest of America to struggle with skyrocketing costs.

For too long, this debate has been stunted by what I call the smallness of our politics – the idea that there isn't much we can agree on or do about the major challenges facing our country. And when some try to propose something bold, the interests groups and the partisans treat it like a sporting event, with each side keeping score of who's up and who's down, using fear and divisiveness and other cheap tricks to win their argument, even if we lose our solution in the process.

Well we can't afford another disappointing charade in 2008. It's not only tiresome, it's wrong. Wrong when businesses have to lay off one employee because they can't afford the health care of another. Wrong when a parent cannot take a sick child to the doctor because they cannot afford the bill that comes with it. Wrong when 46 million Americans have no health care at all. In a country that spends more on health care than any other nation on Earth, it's just wrong.

And yet, in recent years, what's caught the attention of those who haven't always been in favour of reform is the realization that this crisis isn't just morally offensive, it's economically untenable. For years, the can't-do crowd has scared the American people into believing that universal health care would mean socialized medicine and burdensome taxes – that we should just stay out of the way and tinker at the margins...

Well the sceptics must be living somewhere else. Because when you see what the health care crisis is doing to our families, to our economy, to our country, you realize that caution is what's costly. Inaction is what's risky. Doing nothing is what's impossible when it comes to health care in America...

It's time to act. This isn't a problem of money, this is a problem of will. A failure of leadership. We already spend $2.2 trillion a year on health care in this country...

Declaring his Candidacy to Stand for the 2008 US Presidential Election
10 February 2007, Old State Capitol Building, Springfield, Illinois

In February 2007, Barack Obama announced that he would be running for the Democratic Party nomination for the next US presidential election, to be held in November 2008. He made his declaration in the freezing cold outside the Old State Capitol Building in Springfield, Illinois. Here he invokes – as so often before and since – Abraham Lincoln (who made his famous 'House Divided' speech on the same spot in 1858) and Martin Luther King, Jr. At this pivotal moment in his career, Obama produces a speech fit for the occasion. Central to the structure are the words 'Let us…' or 'Let's', which he uses on 27 occasions. Also striking is the emphasis on the first person plural – it is 'we' (Obama and the American people) who are in the contest together. He invokes the memory of King in a sentence that plays on the civil rights leader's surname without actually naming him – this is a form of antonomasia (the identification of a person or thing by reference to some outstanding characteristic or quality). He uses the same figure of speech later when he refers to Lincoln as 'a tall, gangly, self-made Springfield lawyer'; this has a double resonance, because the same description could equally be applied to Obama – height: 1.88m (6ft 2in) – himself. And then Obama makes the announcement that the audience has come to hear. After that, there are several more 'we's before the address reaches its climax in three short declarations beginning with 'I'.

... We all made this journey for a reason. It's humbling, but in my heart I know you didn't come here just for me, you came here because you believe in what this country can be. In the face of war, you believe there can be peace. In the face of despair, you believe there can be hope. In the face of a politics that's shut you out, that's told you to settle, that's divided us for too long, you believe we can be one people, reaching for what's possible, building that more perfect union...

It was here, in Springfield, where North, South, East and West come together that I was reminded of the essential decency of the American people – where I came to believe that through this decency, we can build a more hopeful America.

And that is why, in the shadow of the Old State Capitol, where Lincoln once called on a divided house to stand together, where common hopes and common dreams still live, I stand before you today to announce my candidacy for President of the United States.

I recognize there is a certain presumptuousness – a certain audacity – to this announcement. I know I haven't spent a lot of time learning the ways of Washington. But I've been there long enough to know that the ways of Washington must change.

The genius of our Founders [the Founding Fathers who helped shape the Constitution] is that they designed a system of government that can be changed. And we should take heart, because we've changed this country before. In the face of tyranny, a band of patriots brought an Empire [the British Empire] to its knees. In the face of secession, we unified a nation and set the captives free. In the face of Depression, we put people back to work and lifted millions out of poverty. We welcomed immigrants to our shores, we opened railroads to the west, we landed a man on the moon, and we heard a King's call to let justice roll down like water, and righteousness like a mighty stream.

Each and every time, a new generation has risen up and done what's needed to be done. Today we are called once more – and it is time for our generation to answer that call.

Let's be the generation that ends poverty in America. Every single person willing to work should be able to get job training that leads to a job, and earn a living wage that can pay the bills, and afford child care so their kids have a safe place to go when they work. Let's do this.

Let's be the generation that finally tackles our health care crisis. We can control costs by focusing on prevention, by providing better treatment to the chronically ill, and using technology to cut the bureaucracy. Let's be the generation that says right here, right now, that we will have universal health care in America by the end of the next president's first term.

Let's be the generation that finally frees America from the tyranny of oil. We can harness homegrown, alternative fuels like ethanol and spur the production of more fuel-efficient cars. We can set up a system for capping

greenhouse gases. We can turn this crisis of global warming into a moment of opportunity for innovation, and job creation, and an incentive for businesses that will serve as a model for the world. Let's be the generation that makes future generations proud of what we did here.

Most of all, let's be the generation that never forgets what happened on that September day [11 September 2001; the destruction of the World Trade Center] and confront the terrorists with everything we've got. Politics doesn't have to divide us on this anymore – we can work together to keep our country safe. I've worked with Republican Senator Dick Lugar [from Indiana] to pass a law that will secure and destroy some of the world's deadliest, unguarded weapons. We can work together to track terrorists down with a stronger military, we can tighten the net around their finances, and we can improve our intelligence capabilities. But let us also understand that ultimate victory against our enemies will come only by rebuilding our alliances and exporting those ideals that bring hope and opportunity to millions around the globe.

But all of this cannot come to pass until we bring an end to this war in Iraq. Most of you know I opposed this war from the start. I thought it was a tragic mistake. Today we grieve for the families who have lost loved ones, the hearts that have been broken, and the young lives that could have been. America, it's time to start bringing our troops home. It's time to admit that no amount of American lives can resolve the political disagreement that lies at the heart of someone else's civil war. That's why I have a plan that will bring our combat troops home by March of 2008. Letting the Iraqis know that we will not be there forever is our last, best hope to pressure the Sunni and Shia to come to the table and find peace.

Finally, there is one other thing that is not too late to get right about this war – and that is the homecoming of the men and women – our veterans – who have sacrificed the most. Let us honour their valour by providing the care they need and rebuilding the military they love. Let us be the generation that begins this work...

By ourselves, this change will not happen. Divided, we are bound to fail.

But the life of a tall, gangly, self-made Springfield lawyer tells us that a different future is possible.

He tells us that there is power in words.

He tells us that there is power in conviction.

That beneath all the differences of race and region, faith and station, we are one people.

He tells us that there is power in hope...

And if you will join me in this improbable quest, if you feel destiny calling, and see as I see, a future of endless possibility stretching before us; if you sense, as I sense, that the time is now to shake off our slumber, and slough off our fear, and make good on the debt we owe past and future generations, then I'm ready to take up

the cause, and march with you, and work with you.
Together, starting today, let us finish the work that
needs to be done, and usher in a new birth of freedom
on this Earth.

'Turn the Page' Speech: California Democratic National Convention
28 April 2007, San Diego, California

Addressing the California Democratic National Convention, Barack Obama goes over much of the autobiographical material that was now familiar to his bedrock supporters by way of introducing himself to the much wider audience he had gained since announcing his intention to run for the party's nomination. Known as the 'Turn the Page' speech – he employs the phrase 15 times – it is here that Obama first uses the expression: 'When I am President...'.

... People would ask me... 'You seem like a nice young man... why would you wanna go into something dirty and nasty like politics?'

And I understand the question, and the cynicism. We all understand it.

We understand it because we get the sense today that politics has become a business and not a mission. In the last several years, we have seen Washington become a place where keeping score of who's up and who's down is more important than who's working on behalf of the American people.

We have been told that our mounting debts don't matter, that the economy is doing great, and so Americans should be left to face their anxiety about rising health care costs and disappearing pensions on their own.

We've been told that climate change is a hoax, that our broken schools cannot be fixed, that we are destined to send millions of dollars a day to Mideast dictators for their oil. And we've seen how a foreign policy based on bluster and bombast can lead us into a war that should've never been authorized and never been waged.

And when we try to have an honest debate about the crises we face... the conversation isn't about finding common ground, it's about finding someone to blame. We're divided into Red States [Republicans] and Blue States [Democrats], and told to always point the finger at somebody else – the other party, or gay people, or immigrants.

For good reason, the rest of us have become cynical about what politics can achieve in this country, and as we've turned away in frustration, we know what's filled the void. The lobbyists and influence-peddlers with the cash and the connections – the ones who've turned government into a game only they can afford to play.

They write the cheques and you get stuck with the bills, they get the access while you get to write a letter, they think they own this government, but we're here to tell them it's not for sale. People tell me I haven't spent a lot of time learning the ways of Washington. But I promise you this – I've been there long enough to know that the ways of Washington must change. I'm running for President because the time for the can't-do, won't-do, won't-even-try style of politics is over. It's time to turn the page. There is an awakening taking place in America today. From New Hampshire to California, from Texas to Iowa, we are seeing crowds we've never seen before; we're seeing people showing up to the very first political event of their lives.

They're coming because they know we are at a crossroads right now. Because we are facing a set of challenges we haven't seen in a generation – and if we don't meet those challenges, we could end up leaving our children a world that's a little poorer and a little meaner than we found it.

And so the American people are hungry for a different kind of politics – the kind of politics based on the ideals this country was founded upon. The idea that we are all connected as one people. That we all have a stake in one another.

And so if we do not change our politics – if we do not fundamentally change the way Washington works – then the problems we've been talking about for the last generation will be the same ones that haunt us for generations to come.

We must find a way to come together in this country – to realize that the responsibility we have to one another as Americans is greater than the pursuit of any ideological agenda or corporate bottom line. Democrats of California, it's time to turn the page.

It's time to turn the page on health care... When I am President, I will sign a universal health care law by the end of my first term. My plan will cover the uninsured by letting people buy into the same kind of health care plan that members of Congress give themselves. It will bring down costs by investing in information technology, and preventative care, and by stopping the drug companies from price-gouging when patients need their medicine.

It will help business and families shoulder the burden of catastrophic care so that an illness doesn't lead to a bankruptcy. And it will save the average family a thousand dollars a year on their premiums. We can do this.

It's time to turn the page on education – to move past the slow decay of indifference that says some schools can't be fixed and some kids just can't learn.

As President, I will launch a campaign to recruit and support hundreds of thousands of new teachers across the country, because the most important part of any education is the person standing in the front of the classroom. It's time to treat teaching like the profession it is – paying teachers what they deserve and working with them – not against them – to develop the high standards we need. We can do this.

It's time to turn the page on energy – to break the political stalemate that's kept our fuel efficiency standards in the same place for 20 years; to tell the oil and auto industries that they must act, not only because their future's at stake, but because the future of our country and our planet is at stake as well.

As President, I will institute a cap-and-trade system that would dramatically reduce carbon emissions and auction off emissions credits that would generate millions of dollars to invest in renewable sources of energy. I'll put in place a low-carbon fuel standard like you have here in California that will take 32 million cars' worth of pollution off the road. And I'd raise the fuel efficiency standards for our cars and trucks because we know we have the technology to do it and it's time we did. We can do this.

We can do all of this. But most of all, we have to turn the page on this disaster in Iraq and restore our standing in the world. I am proud that I stood up in 2002 and urged our leaders not to take us down this dangerous path. And so many of you did the same, even when it wasn't popular to do so.

We knew back then this war was a mistake. We knew back then that it was dangerous diversion from the struggle against the terrorists who attacked us on September 11th. We knew back then that we could find ourselves in an occupation of undetermined length, at undetermined cost, with undetermined consequences.

But the war went forward. And now, we've seen those consequences and we mourn for the dead and wounded...

It's time to turn the page for hope. It's time to turn the page for justice. It is time to turn the page and write the next chapter in the great American story. Let's begin the work. Let's do this together. Let's turn that page. Thank you.

Chapter 4

THE MAKING OF HISTORY: 44TH PRESIDENT OF THE UNITED STATES
(2008–2009)

The race for the Democratic nomination had many ups and downs, and it was not clear until June 2008 which of the last two contenders would win it – Barack Obama or Hillary Clinton, the US senator from New York and wife of former President Bill Clinton (1993–2001). At the end of August, Obama was formally adopted as the Democratic presidential candidate and then went head to head with the Republican nominee, John McCain. Within the Democratic ranks, hope was higher than expectation, as many feared that their vote would be fatally reduced as Clinton supporters shunned Obama and white Southerners refused to vote for an African American. Through it all, Obama held firmly to his belief, first stated in his nomination acceptance speech (page 112) that 'You make a big election about small things'. On 4 November he won convincingly, carrying 28 of the 50 states and securing 52.9 per cent of the vote.

'Yes We Can': Super Tuesday

5 February 2008, Chicago, Illinois

Super Tuesday is the day in every presidential election year when the greatest number of US states hold primary elections to select their delegates to the national conventions at which each party's candidates are officially nominated. In 2008, 24 states held primaries or caucuses on this date, with just over half of all pledged Democratic Party delegates being selected. It was in this speech that Barack Obama introduced the slogan 'Yes we can'. He spoke before knowing whether he had won the nomination.

... But there is one thing on this February night that we do not need the final results to know – our time has come, our movement is real, and change is coming to America...

What began as a whisper in Springfield [page 87] has swelled to a chorus of millions calling for change. A chorus that cannot be ignored. That cannot be deterred. This time can be different because this campaign for the presidency is different.

It's different not because of me, but because of you. Because you are tired of being disappointed and tired of being let down. You're tired of hearing promises made and plans proposed in the heat of a campaign only to have nothing change when everyone goes back to Washington...

But in this election – at this moment – you are standing up all across this country to say, not this time. Not this year. The stakes are too high and the challenges too great to play the same Washington game with the same Washington players and expect a different result. This time must be different.

Now, this isn't about me and it's not about Senator Clinton...

But this fall we owe the American people a real choice. It's change versus more of the same. It's the future versus the past...

It's a choice between having a debate with the other party about who has the most experience in Washington, or having one about who's most likely to change Washington. Because that's a debate we can win.

It's a choice between a candidate [Clinton] who's taken more money from Washington lobbyists than either Republican in this race, and a campaign that hasn't taken a dime of their money because we've been funded by you... [Obama was the first serious presidential candidate in US history whose election funds were raised almost entirely from small donations by private individuals.]

When I am President, we will put an end to a politics that uses 9/11 [terrorist attacks on the United States, 11 September 2001] as a way to scare up votes, and start seeing it as a challenge that should unite America and the world against the common threats of the 21st century: terrorism and nuclear weapons; climate change and poverty; genocide and disease.

We can do this. It will not be easy. It will require struggle and sacrifice. There will be setbacks and we will make mistakes. And that is why we need all the help we can get. So tonight I want to speak directly to all those Americans who have yet to join this movement but still hunger for change – we need you. We need you to stand with us, and work with us, and help us prove that together, ordinary people can still do extraordinary things...

We are the ones we've been waiting for. We are the change that we seek. We are the hope of those boys who have little; who've been told that they cannot have what they dream; that they cannot be what they imagine.

Yes they can.

We are the hope of the father who goes to work before dawn and lies awake with doubts that tell him he cannot give his children the same opportunities that someone gave him.

Yes he can.

We are the hope of the woman who hears that her city will not be rebuilt; that she cannot reclaim the life that was swept away in a terrible storm.

Yes she can.

We are the hope of the future; the answer to the cynics who tell us our house must stand divided; that we cannot come together; that we cannot remake this world as it should be.

Because we know what we have seen and what we
believe – that what began as a whisper has now swelled
to a chorus that cannot be ignored; that will not be
deterred; that will ring out across this land as a hymn
that will heal this nation, repair this world, and make
this time different than all the rest – Yes. We. Can.

Primary Night: Texas and Ohio

4 March 2008, San Antonio, Texas

Still uncertain of the Democratic nomination,
Barack Obama turns to criticisms voiced by his
main current rival, Hillary Clinton, and, he hopes, his
next one, Republican presidential nominee Senator
John McCain. His rebuttals all begin with the same
phrase – 'There's nothing empty about...' – and his
restatements of his own position all start with the
inclusive 'We believe'. He ends with the words that had
by now become a catchphrase; 'Yes we can'.

... We want a new course for this country. We want new
leadership in Washington. We want change in America.

John McCain and Senator Clinton echo each other in
dismissing this call for change. They say it is eloquent
but empty; speeches and not solutions...

They should know that there's nothing empty about the
call for affordable health care that came from the young
student who told me she gets three hours of sleep
because she works the night shift after a full day of
college and still can't pay her sister's medical bills.

There's nothing empty about the call for help that came
from the mother in San Antonio who saw her mortgage
double in two weeks and didn't know where her two-
year-olds would sleep at night when they were kicked
out of their home.

There's nothing empty about the call for change
that came from the elderly woman who wants it so
badly that she sent me an envelope with a money
order for $3.01 and a simple verse of scripture
tucked inside...

We... believe that there is a larger responsibility we
have to one another as Americans...

We believe that a child born tonight should have the
same chances whether she arrives in the barrios of San
Antonio or the suburbs of St. Louis; on the streets of
Chicago or the hills of Appalachia...

And if that child should ever get the chance to travel
the world, and someone should ask her where she is
from, we believe that she should always be able to hold
her head high with pride in her voice when she answers
'I am an American'.

That is the course we seek. That is the change we are
calling for. You can call it many things, but you cannot
call it empty...

Can we come together across party and region; race and
religion to restore prosperity and opportunity as the
birthright of every American?

Can we lead the community of nations in taking on the
common threats of the 21st century – terrorism and
climate change; genocide and disease?

Can we send a message to all those weary travellers
beyond our shores who long to be free from fear and
want that the United States of America is, and always
will be, 'the last best, hope of Earth'?

We say; we hope; we believe – yes we can.

'A More Perfect Union'

18 March 2008, Philadelphia, Pennsylvania

**In March 2008, Obama made a speech in which he
sought to distance himself from his former pastor,
the Reverend Jeremiah Wright, who had attracted
intense publicity by remarks that were widely
construed to imply that the United States had brought
the terrorist attacks of 11 September 2001 on itself. The
presidential candidate re-emphasized the homogeneity
of the aspirations of all US citizens, regardless of their
ethnic antecedents.**

I believe deeply that we cannot solve the challenges of
our time unless we solve them together – unless we
perfect our union by understanding that we may have
different stories, but we hold common hopes; that we
may not look the same and we may not have come
from the same place, but we all want to move in the
same direction – towards a better future for our
children and our grandchildren...

I can no more disown him [Wright] than I can disown
the black community. I can no more disown him than I
can my white grandmother – a woman who helped raise
me, a woman who sacrificed again and again for me, a
woman who loves me as much as she loves anything in
this world, but a woman who once confessed her fear of
black men who passed by her on the street, and who on
more than one occasion has uttered racial or ethnic
stereotypes that made me cringe...

I have asserted a firm conviction – a conviction rooted
in my faith in God and my faith in the American people
– that working together we can move beyond some of
our old racial wounds, and that in fact we have no
choice if we are to continue on the path of a more
perfect union.

For the African American community, that path means
embracing the burdens of our past without becoming
victims of our past. It means continuing to insist on a
full measure of justice in every aspect of American life.
But it also means binding our particular grievances –
for better health care, and better schools, and better jobs
– to the larger aspirations of all Americans – the white
woman struggling to break the glass ceiling, the white
man who's been laid off, the immigrant trying to feed
his family. And it means taking full responsibility for
our own lives – by demanding more from our fathers,
and spending more time with our children, and reading
to them, and teaching them that while they may face
challenges and discrimination in their own lives, they
must never succumb to despair or cynicism; they must
always believe that they can write their own destiny...

The profound mistake of Reverend Wright's sermons is not that he spoke about racism in our society. It's that he spoke as if our society was static; as if no progress has been made; as if this country – a country that has made it possible for one of his own members to run for the highest office in the land and build a coalition of white and black, Latino and Asian, rich and poor, young and old – is still irrevocably bound to a tragic past. But what we know – what we have seen – is that America can change. That is the true genius of this nation. What we have already achieved gives us hope – the audacity to hope – for what we can and must achieve tomorrow.

In the white community, the path to a more perfect union means acknowledging that what ails the African American community does not just exist in the minds of black people; that the legacy of discrimination – and current incidents of discrimination, while less overt than in the past – are real and must be addressed...

In the end, then, what is called for is nothing more, and nothing less, than what all the world's great religions demand – that we do unto others as we would have them do unto us. Let us be our brother's keeper, Scripture tells us. Let us be our sister's keeper. Let us find that common stake we all have in one another, and let our politics reflect that spirit as well...

I would not be running for President if I didn't believe with all my heart that this is what the vast majority of Americans want for this country. This union may never be perfect, but generation after generation has shown that it can always be perfected. And today, whenever I find myself feeling doubtful or cynical about this possibility, what gives me the most hope is the next generation – the young people whose attitudes and beliefs and openness to change have already made history in this election…

Line on US Human Rights Violations

13 April 2008, Messiah College, Philadelphia, Pennsylvania

As the War on Terror continued, it came to worldwide attention that the United States had authorized the kidnapping of suspects who were then transported to foreign countries – notably Egypt, Pakistan, Poland and Syria – to be interrogated brutally; the process was known as extraordinary rendition. When asked about this policy at the 2008 Democratic Compassion Forum, Barack Obama did not mince his words.

We have to be clear and unequivocal. We do not torture, period. Our government does not torture. That should be our position. That will be my position as president. That includes renditions. We don't farm out torture. We don't subcontract torture.

Speech at AP Annual Luncheon

14 April 2008, Washington, D.C.

In the first week of April, Barack Obama – normally so sure-footed politically – made a gaffe. Characterizing working-class people who have lost their jobs, he said:

'They get bitter, they cling to guns or religion or antipathy to people who aren't like them or anti-immigrant sentiment or anti-trade sentiment, as a way to explain their frustrations.' He took the following speech to the journalists of Associated Press (AP) as an opportunity to repair the damage; having done that, he turned on his Republican rival, John McCain, and ended right back on message – the message of hope.

Good afternoon. I know I kept a lot of you guys busy this weekend with the comments I made last week. Some of you might even be a little bitter about that.

As I said yesterday, I regret some of the words I chose, partly because the way that these remarks have been interpreted have offended some people and partly because they have served as one more distraction from the critical debate that we must have in this election season.

I'm a person of deep faith, and my religion has sustained me through a lot in my life. I even gave a speech on faith before I ever started running for President where I said that Democrats, 'make a mistake when we fail to acknowledge the power of faith in people's lives'. I also represent a state with a large number of hunters and sportsmen, and I understand how important these traditions are to families in Illinois and all across America. And, contrary to what my poor word choices may have implied or my opponents have suggested, I've never believed that these traditions or people's faith has anything to do with how much money they have.

But I will never walk away from the larger point that I was trying to make. For the last several decades, people in small towns and cities and rural areas all across this country have seen globalization change the rules of the game on them...

I may have made a mistake last week in the words that I chose, but the other party has made a much more damaging mistake in the failed policies they've chosen and the bankrupt philosophy they've embraced for the last three decades...

The other side is still betting that the American people won't notice that John McCain is running for George Bush's third term. They think that they'll forget about all that's happened in the last eight years; that they'll be tricked into believing that it's either me or our party that is the one that's out of touch with what's going on in their lives.

Well I'm making a different bet. I'm betting on the American people.

The men and women I've met in small towns and big cities across this country see this election as a defining moment in our history. They understand what's at stake here because they're living it every day. And they are tired of being distracted by fake controversies. They are fed up with politicians trying to divide us for their own political gain. And I believe they'll see through the tactics that are used every year, in every election, to appeal to our fears, or our biases, or our differences – because they've never wanted or needed change as badly as they do now...

'The American Promise': Acceptance Speech at the Democratic Convention

28 August 2008, Mile High Stadium, Denver, Colorado

Having beaten all-comers for the nomination, Barack Obama was formally adopted as the Democratic candidate for the 2008 US presidential election. He began his speech by acknowledging his rivals, particularly his strongest opponent, Hillary Clinton, and Joe Biden, whom Obama had adopted six days previously as his vice-presidential running mate. He then paid a brief tribute to his wife, Michelle, and their children, Sasha and Malia, before launching into his key messages. Note the stress on immediacy, especially in the repeated phrase 'Now is the time', and the reference back to 'enough' (page 52).

... America, now is not the time for small plans. Now is the time to finally meet our moral obligation to provide every child a world-class education, because it will take nothing less to compete in the global economy. Michelle and I are only here tonight because we were given a chance at an education. And I will not settle for an America where some kids don't have that chance. I'll invest in early childhood education. I'll recruit an army of new teachers, and pay them higher salaries and give them more support. And in exchange, I'll ask for higher standards and more accountability. And we will keep our promise to every young American – if you commit to serving your community or your country, we will make sure you can afford a college education.

Now is the time to finally keep the promise of affordable, accessible health care for every single American. If you have health care, my plan will lower your premiums. If you don't, you'll be able to get the same kind of coverage that members of Congress give themselves. And as someone who watched my mother argue with insurance companies while she lay in bed dying of cancer, I will make certain those companies stop discriminating against those who are sick and need care the most.

Now is the time to help families with paid sick days and better family leave, because nobody in America should have to choose between keeping their jobs and caring for a sick child or ailing parent.

Now is the time to change our bankruptcy laws, so that your pensions are protected ahead of CEO bonuses; and the time to protect Social Security for future generations.

And now is the time to keep the promise of equal pay for an equal day's work, because I want my daughters to have exactly the same opportunities as your sons...

You make a big election about small things...

For eighteen long months, you have stood up, one by one, and said 'Enough' to the politics of the past. You understand that in this election, the greatest risk we can take is to try the same old politics with the same old players and expect a different result. You have shown what history teaches us – that at defining moments like this one, the change we need doesn't come from Washington. Change comes to Washington. Change happens because the American people demand it – because they rise up and insist on new ideas and new leadership, a new politics for a new time.

America, this is one of those moments...

America, we cannot turn back. Not with so much work to be done. Not with so many children to educate, and so many veterans to care for. Not with an economy to fix and cities to rebuild and farms to save. Not with so many families to protect and so many lives to mend. America, we cannot turn back. We cannot walk alone. At this moment, in this election, we must pledge once more to march into the future. Let us keep that promise – that American promise – and in the words of Scripture [Hebrews 10:23] hold firmly, without wavering, to the hope that we confess.

Second Presidential Debate: Barack Obama vs John McCain

7 October 2008, Belmont University, Nashville, Tennessee

After the main parties had chosen their presidential nominees, the two candidates went head to head in three debates broadcast live on radio and television. The first, at the University of Mississippi on 26 September, was adjudged fairly even, with Barack Obama ahead on the economy and John McCain sounding better than his opponent on foreign policy. Opinion polls put Obama ahead in the next two debates, held at Belmont University in Nashville, Tennessee, on 7 October, and at Hofstra University on Long Island, New York, on 15 October.

This extract shows how, although there was often little to choose between the rivals in terms of substance, Obama, here through his use of the words 'critical', 'challenge' and 'opportunity', presented his ideas with greater dynamism than McCain.

TOM BROKAW [NBC news journalist]: What would you do for the environment?

OBAMA: It is critical that we understand this is not just a challenge, it's an opportunity, because if we create a new energy economy, we can create five million new jobs, easily. It can be an engine that drives us into the future the same way the computer was the engine for economic growth over the last couple of decades. We can do it, but we're going to have to make an investment. The same way the computer was originally invented by a bunch of government scientists who were trying to figure out, for defence purposes, how to communicate, we've got to understand that this is a national security issue, as well.

McCAIN: We can move forward, and clean up our climate, and develop green technologies, and alternative energies for battery-powered cars, so that we can clean up our environment and at the same time get our economy going by creating millions of jobs.

The Night Before the Election

3 November 2008, Manassas, Prince William County, Virginia

At 10:30, on the night before the 2008 US presidential election, Barack Obama addressed a rally of his supporters in Manassas, Virginia. The speech was a tour de force that demonstrated his capacity to reach a wide audience while keeping his subject matter focused on the people in front of him and on local issues. On first hearing, the 'fired up' anecdote sounds trivial, perhaps almost to a fault. But it encapsulates the Senator's appeal as a candidate whose world-attitude and policies have grown out of listening to the real concerns of ordinary people – as he said (page 112), 'You make a big election about small things.'

What a scene. What a crowd. Thank you for Virginia. [Crowd chants 'Yes we can'.]

Let me start by noting, Virginia, that this is our last rally. This is the last rally of a campaign that began nearly two years ago…

I just want to say that whatever happens tomorrow, I have been deeply humbled by this journey…

You have enriched my life, you have moved me again and again. You have inspired me. Sometimes when I have been down you have lifted me up. You filled me with new hope for our future and you have reminded me about what makes America so special…

I come away with an unyielding belief that if we only had a government as responsible as all of you, as compassionate as the American people, that there is no obstacle that we can't overcome. There is no destiny that we cannot fulfil.

Virginia, I have just one word for you, just one word. Tomorrow. Tomorrow. After decades of broken politics in Washington, 8 years of failed policies from George Bush, 21 months of campaigning, we are less than one day away from bringing about change in America.

Tomorrow you can turn the page on policies that put greed and irresponsibility before hard work and sacrifice. Tomorrow you can choose policies that invest in our middle class, create new jobs and grow this economy so that everybody has a chance to succeed... Tomorrow you can put an end to the politics that would divide a nation just to win an election; that puts reason against reason, and city against town, Republican against Democrat; that asks us to fear at a time when we need to hope.

Tomorrow, at this defining moment in history, you can give this country the change that we need. It starts here in Virginia. It starts here in Manassas. This is where change begins...

In this campaign I have had the privilege to witness what is best in America, in the stories, in the faces, of men and women I have met at countless rallies, town hall meetings, VFW [Veterans of Foreign Wars; a charity] halls, living rooms, diners, all across America, men and women who shared with me their stories and spoke of their struggles but they also spoke of their hopes and dreams. They want for their children a sense of obligation and debts to be paid to earlier generations.

I met one of those women in Greenwood, South Carolina... I turned to her and I said: 'I really want your endorsement.' And she looked at me and she said: 'I'll tell you what, Obama, I will give you my endorsement if you come to my hometown of Greenwood, South Carolina.' I must have had a sip of wine or something that night because right away I said: 'Okay. I'm coming.'

So the next time I come to South Carolina it's about a month later. We fly in about midnight. We get to the hotel about one o'clock in the morning. I'm exhausted. I'm dragging my bags to my room when I get a tap on my shoulder and I look back and it is one of my staff people who says: 'Senator we need to be out of the hotel by 6 a.m.' I say, 'Why is that?' He says, 'Because we have to go to Greenwood, like you promised.'

So the next morning I wake up and I feel terrible, and I think I am coming down with a cold, my back is sore, I feel worse than when I went to bed. I open up the curtains in the hotel room to get some sunlight in and hopefully wake me up, but it's pouring down rain...

We drive, and we drive, and we drive. It turns out that Greenwood is about an hour and a half from everywhere else. Finally we get to Greenwood.

First of all you do not know you're in Greenwood when you get to Greenwood.... We pull off to a small building – a little field house in a park – and we go inside, and low and behold, after an hour and a half drive, turns out there are twenty people there. Twenty people. They look all kind of damp and sleepy, maybe they aren't really excited to be there either.

But I am a professional, I've got to do what I got to do. I'm going around, I'm shaking hands, I am saying: 'How are you doing? What are you doing?'

As I go around the room suddenly I hear this voice cry out behind me 'Fired up'. I'm shocked. I jumped up. I don't know what is going on. But everyone else acts as though this were normal and they say 'fired up'. Then I hear this voice say 'Ready to go'. And the 20 people in the room act like this happens all the time and they say 'Ready to go'.

I don't know what's going on so I looked behind me and there is this small woman, about 60 years old, a little over 5 feet, looks like she just came from church – she's got on a big church hat. She's standing there, she looks at me and she smiles and she says, 'Fired up'.

It turns out that she was a city Councilwoman from Greenwood who also moonlights as a private detective. I'm not making this up. And it turns out that she is famous for her chant. She does this wherever she goes. She says 'Fired up' and the people say 'Fired up', and she says 'Ready to go' and they say 'Ready to go'.

For the next five minutes she proceeds to do this. 'Fired up?' and everyone says 'Fired up' and she says 'Ready to go' and they say 'Ready to go'. I'm standing there and

I'm thinking I'm being outflanked by this woman. She's stealing my thunder. I look at my staff and they shrugged their shoulders, they don't know how long this is going to go on.

But here's the thing, Virginia. After a minute or so I am feeling kind of fired up. I'm feeling like I'm ready to go. So I join in the chant. It feels good...

That's how this thing started. It shows you what one voice can do. That one voice can change a room. And if a voice can change a room, it can change a city, and if it can change a city, it can change a state, and if it can change a state, it can change a nation, and if it can change a nation, it can change the world.

Virginia, your voice can change the world tomorrow. In 21 hours if you are willing to endure some rain, if you are willing to drag that person you know who is not going to vote, to the polls. If you are willing to organize and volunteer in the offices, if you are willing to stand with me, if you are willing to fight with me, I know your voice will matter.

So I have just one question for you Virginia: are you fired up? Ready to go? Fired up. Ready to go. Fired up. Ready to go. Fired up. Ready to go.

Virginia, let's go change the world. God bless you and God bless the United States of America.

Presidential Election Night: Victory Speech

4 November 2008, Grant Park, Chicago, Illinois

On 4 November 2008, Barack Obama became President-elect of the United States. As the first African American president, Obama made history. Millions of people around the world watched as Obama made the following speech; some, like Rev. Jesse Jackson (African American Democrat politician who ran for the White House in 1984 and 1988), were in tears. The speech has been hailed as one of the best of its kind and certainly one of Barack Obama's finest.

If there is anyone out there who still doubts that America is a place where all things are possible; who still wonders if the dream of our founders is alive in our time; who still questions the power of our democracy, tonight is your answer.

It's the answer told by lines that stretched around schools and churches in numbers this nation has never seen; by people who waited three hours and four hours, many for the very first time in their lives, because they believed that this time must be different; that their voice could be that difference.

It's the answer spoken by young and old, rich and poor, Democrat and Republican, black, white, Latino, Asian, Native American, gay, straight, disabled and not disabled Americans who sent a message to the world that we have never been a collection of Red States and Blue States: we are, and always will be, the United States of America.

It's the answer that led those who have been told for so long by so many to be cynical, and fearful, and doubtful of what we can achieve to put their hands on the arc of history and bend it once more toward the hope of a better day.

It's been a long time coming, but tonight, because of what we did on this day, in this election, at this defining moment, change has come to America...

Above all, I will never forget who this victory truly belongs to – it belongs to you.

I was never the likeliest candidate for this office. We didn't start with much money or many endorsements...

It was built by working men and women who dug into what little savings they had to give five dollars and ten dollars and twenty dollars to this cause. It grew strength from the young people who rejected the myth of their generation's apathy...

The road ahead will be long. Our climb will be steep. We may not get there in one year or even one term, but America – I have never been more hopeful than I am tonight that we will get there. I promise you – we as a people will get there...

For that is the true genius of America – that America can change. Our union can be perfected. And what we have already achieved gives us hope for what we can and must achieve tomorrow.

This election had many firsts and many stories that will be told for generations. But one that's on my mind tonight is about a woman who cast her ballot in Atlanta. She's a lot like the millions of others who stood in line to make their voice heard in this election except for one thing – Ann Nixon Cooper is 106 years old.

She was born just a generation past slavery; a time when there were no cars on the road or planes in the sky; when someone like her couldn't vote for two reasons – because she was a woman and because of the colour of her skin.

And tonight, I think about all that she's seen throughout her century in America – the heartache and the hope; the struggle and the progress; the times we were told that we can't, and the people who pressed on with that American creed: Yes we can.

And tonight, I think about all that she's seen throughout her century in America – the heartache and the hope; the struggle and the progress; the times we were told that we can't, and the people who pressed on with that American creed: Yes we can.

At a time when women's voices were silenced and their hopes dismissed, she lived to see them stand up and speak out and reach for the ballot. Yes we can.

When there was despair in the dust bowl and depression across the land, she saw a nation conquer fear itself with a New Deal, new jobs and a new sense of common purpose. Yes we can.

When the bombs fell on our harbour and tyranny
threatened the world, she was there to witness a
generation rise to greatness and a democracy was saved.
Yes we can.

She was there for the buses in Montgomery, the hoses
in Birmingham, a bridge in Selma, and a preacher from
Atlanta who told a people that 'We Shall Overcome'. Yes
we can.

A man touched down on the moon, a wall came down
in Berlin, a world was connected by our own science
and imagination. And this year, in this election, she
touched her finger to a screen, and cast her vote,
because after 106 years in America, through the best of
times and the darkest of hours, she knows how America
can change. Yes we can.

America, we have come so far. We have seen so much.
But there is so much more to do. So tonight, let us ask
ourselves – if our children should live to see the next
century; if my daughters should be so lucky to live as
long as Ann Nixon Cooper, what change will they see?
What progress will we have made?

This is our chance to answer that call. This is our
moment. This is our time – to put our people back to
work and open doors of opportunity for our kids;
to restore prosperity and promote the cause of peace;
to reclaim the American Dream and reaffirm that
fundamental truth – that out of many, we are one; that
while we breathe, we hope, and where we are met with
cynicism, and doubt, and those who tell us that we

can't, we will respond with that timeless creed that sums up the spirit of a people:

Yes We Can. Thank you, God bless you, and may God Bless the United States of America.

Time Magazine Interview

5 December 2008, Chicago, Illinois

As Barack Obama prepared to take the reins of office, he was asked: 'When voters look at your Administration two years from now... how will they know whether you're succeeding?' His answer was risky because it may come back to haunt him but in the short term it appeared refreshingly honest and straightforward.

I think there are a couple of benchmarks we've set for ourselves during the course of this campaign. On [domestic] policy, have we helped this economy recover from what is the worst financial crisis since the Great Depression? Have we instituted financial regulations and rules of the road that assure this kind of crisis doesn't occur again? Have we created jobs that pay well and allow families to support themselves? Have we made significant progress on reducing the cost of health care and expanding coverage? Have we begun what will probably be a decade-long project to shift America to a new energy economy? Have we begun what may be an even longer project of revitalizing our public [state] school systems so we can compete in the 21st century?...

On foreign policy, have we closed down Guantánamo
[US naval base in Cuba used from 2002 as an internment
facility for alleged Muslim militants detained without
trial during the War on Terror in Afghanistan and Iraq]
in a responsible way, put a clear end to torture and
restored a balance between the demands of our security
and our Constitution? Have we rebuilt alliances around
the world effectively? Have I drawn down US troops out
of Iraq, and have we strengthened our approach in
Afghanistan – not just militarily but also diplomatically
and in terms of development? And have we been able to
reinvigorate international institutions to deal with
transnational threats, like climate change, that we can't
solve on our own?

And outside of specific policy measures, two years from
now, I want the American people to be able to say,
'Government's not perfect; there are some things
Obama does that get on my nerves. But you know
what? I feel like the government's working for me.
I feel like it's accountable. I feel like it's transparent. I
feel that I am well informed about what government
actions are being taken. I feel that this is a President
and an Administration that admits when it makes
mistakes and adapts itself to new information, that
believes in making decisions based on facts and on
science as opposed to what is politically expedient.'
Those are some of the intangibles that I hope people
two years from now can claim.

Inaugural Address

20 January 2009, Capitol Hill, Washington D.C.

Barack Obama's inaugural address was uplifting, as befitted the historic moment when, for the first time, an African American was sworn in to the highest office of a nation whose population of over 300 million includes more than 40 million black people. It was also appropriately muted for an occasion that, despite its pomp and theatricality, was overshadowed by the wars in Iraq and Afghanistan and by a deepening world economic crisis. It was the politics of hope informed by the politics of realism.

Rhetorically, the speech employs some now familiar devices while skilfully approaching others and then, at the last moment, avoiding them. Obama again uses the tricolon device, as for example in his opening line ('humbled', 'grateful', 'mindful') and in the three sentences that begin 'For us...'. Elsewhere, he appears to be going down the same path with repetitions of certain phrases, but then does not deliver the expected third, as in the sections that begin 'The time has come...'.

In this speech, Obama coins some memorable phrases: 'bitter swill' is one; another is 'a nation cannot prosper long when it favours only the prosperous'. The most striking is his challenge to America's enemies: 'We will extend a hand if you are willing to unclench your fist.' However, immediately after Obama finished speaking, the passage highlighted by most on-the-spot commentators was: 'Starting today, we must pick ourselves up, dust ourselves off, and begin again the work of remaking America.'

My fellow citizens:

I stand here today humbled by the task before us, grateful for the trust you have bestowed, mindful of the sacrifices borne by our ancestors. I thank [outgoing] President [George W.] Bush for his service to our nation, as well as the generosity and cooperation he has shown throughout this transition.

Forty-four Americans have now taken the presidential oath. The words have been spoken during rising tides of prosperity and the still waters of peace. Yet, every so often the oath is taken amidst gathering clouds and raging storms. At these moments, America has carried on not simply because of the skill or vision of those in high office, but because we the people have remained faithful to the ideals of our forbears, and true to our founding documents.

So it has been. So it must be with this generation of Americans.

That we are in the midst of crisis is now well understood. Our nation is at war, against a far-reaching network of violence and hatred. Our economy is badly weakened, a consequence of greed and irresponsibility on the part of some, but also our collective failure to make hard choices and prepare the nation for a new age. Homes have been lost; jobs shed; businesses shuttered. Our health care is too costly; our schools fail too many; and each day brings further evidence that the ways we use energy strengthen our adversaries and threaten our planet.

These are the indicators of crisis, subject to data and statistics. Less measurable but no less profound is a sapping of confidence across our land – a nagging fear that America's decline is inevitable, and that the next generation must lower its sights.

Today I say to you that the challenges we face are real. They are serious and they are many. They will not be met easily or in a short span of time. But know this, America – they will be met.

On this day, we gather because we have chosen hope over fear, unity of purpose over conflict and discord.

On this day, we come to proclaim an end to the petty grievances and false promises, the recriminations and worn out dogmas, that for far too long have strangled our politics.

We remain a young nation, but in the words of Scripture [I Corinthians, xiii 11], the time has come to set aside childish things.

The time has come to reaffirm our enduring spirit; to choose our better history; to carry forward that precious gift, that noble idea, passed on from generation to generation: the God-given promise that all are equal, all are free, and all deserve a chance to pursue their full measure of happiness.

In reaffirming the greatness of our nation, we understand that greatness is never a given. It must be earned. Our journey has never been one of short-cuts or settling for less. It has not been the path for the faint-hearted – for those who prefer leisure over work, or seek only the pleasures of riches and fame. Rather, it has been the risk-takers, the doers, the makers of things – some celebrated but more often men and women obscure in their labour, who have carried us up the long, rugged path towards prosperity and freedom.

For us, they packed up their few worldly possessions and travelled across oceans in search of a new life. For us, they toiled in sweatshops and settled the West; endured the lash of the whip and plowed the hard earth.

For us, they fought and died, in places like Concord [site of an American Revolution battle, 1775] and Gettysburg [American Civil War battle, 1863]; Normandy [World War II, 1944] and Khe Sahn [Vietnam War battle, 1968]. Time and again these men and women struggled and sacrificed and worked till their hands were raw so that we might live a better life. They saw America as bigger than the sum of our individual ambitions; greater than all the differences of birth or wealth or faction.

This is the journey we continue today. We remain the most prosperous, powerful nation on Earth. Our workers are no less productive than when this crisis began. Our minds are no less inventive, our goods and services no less needed than they were last week or last month or last year. Our capacity remains undiminished. But our time of standing pat, of protecting narrow interests and putting off unpleasant decisions – that time has surely passed. Starting today, we must pick ourselves up, dust ourselves off, and begin again the work of remaking America.

For everywhere we look, there is work to be done. The state of the economy calls for action, bold and swift, and we will act – not only to create new jobs, but to lay a new foundation for growth. We will build the roads and bridges, the electric grids and digital lines that feed our commerce and bind us together. We will restore science to its rightful place, and wield technology's wonders to raise health care's quality and lower its cost. We will harness the sun and the winds and the soil to fuel our cars and run our factories. And we will transform our schools and colleges and universities to meet the demands of a new age. All this we can do. And all this we will do.

Now, there are some who question the scale of our ambitions – who suggest that our system cannot tolerate too many big plans. Their memories are short. For they have forgotten what this country has already done; what free men and women can achieve when imagination is joined to common purpose, and necessity to courage.

What the cynics fail to understand is that the ground has shifted beneath them – that the stale political arguments that have consumed us for so long no longer apply. The question we ask today is not whether our government is too big or too small, but whether it works – whether it helps families find jobs at a decent wage, care they can afford, a retirement that is dignified. Where the answer is yes, we intend to move forward. Where the answer is no, programmes will end. And those of us who manage the public's dollars will be held to account – to spend wisely, reform bad habits, and do our business in the light of day – because only then can we restore the vital trust between a people and their government.

Nor is the question before us whether the market is a force for good or ill. Its power to generate wealth and expand freedom is unmatched, but this crisis has reminded us that, without a watchful eye, the market can spin out of control – and that a nation cannot prosper long when it favours only the prosperous.

The success of our economy has always depended not just on the size of our Gross Domestic Product, but on the reach of our prosperity; on our ability to extend opportunity to every willing heart – not out of charity, but because it is the surest route to our common good.

As for our common defence, we reject as false the choice between our safety and our ideals. Our Founding Fathers, faced with perils we can scarcely imagine, drafted a charter to assure the rule of law and the rights of man, a charter expanded by the blood of generations. Those ideals still light the world, and we will not give them up for expedience's sake.

And so to all other peoples and governments who are watching today, from the grandest capitals to the small village [in Kenya] where my father was born: know that America is a friend of each nation and every man, woman and child who seeks a future of peace and dignity, and that we are ready to lead once more. Recall that earlier generations faced down fascism and communism not just with missiles and tanks, but with sturdy alliances and enduring convictions. They understood that our power alone cannot protect us, nor does it entitle us to do as we please. Instead, they knew that our power grows through its prudent use; our security emanates from the justness of our cause, the force of our example, the tempering qualities of humility and restraint.

We are the keepers of this legacy. Guided by these principles once more, we can meet those new threats that demand even greater effort – even greater cooperation and understanding between nations. We will begin to responsibly leave Iraq to its people, and forge a hard-earned peace in Afghanistan. With old friends and former foes, we will work tirelessly to lessen the nuclear threat, and roll back the spectre of a warming planet. We will not apologize for our way of life, nor will we waver in its defence, and for those who seek to advance their aims by inducing terror and slaughtering innocents, we say to you now that our spirit is stronger and cannot be broken; you cannot outlast us, and we will defeat you.

For we know that our patchwork heritage is a strength, not a weakness. We are a nation of Christians and Muslims, Jews and Hindus – and non-believers. We are shaped by every language and culture, drawn from every end of this Earth; and because we have tasted the bitter swill of civil war and segregation, and emerged from that dark chapter stronger and more united, we cannot help but believe that the old hatreds shall someday pass; that the lines of tribe shall soon dissolve; that as the world grows smaller, our common humanity shall reveal itself; and that America must play its role in ushering in a new era of peace.

To the Muslim world, we seek a new way forward, based on mutual interest and mutual respect. To those leaders around the globe who seek to sow conflict, or blame their society's ills on the West – know that your people will judge you on what you can build, not what you destroy. To those who cling to power through corruption and deceit and the silencing of dissent, know that you are on the wrong side of history; but that we will extend a hand if you are willing to unclench your fist.

To the people of poor nations, we pledge to work alongside you to make your farms flourish and let clean waters flow; to nourish starved bodies and feed hungry minds. And to those nations like ours that enjoy relative plenty, we say we can no longer afford indifference to suffering outside our borders; nor can we consume the world's resources without regard to effect. For the world has changed, and we must change with it.

As we consider the road that unfolds before us, we remember with humble gratitude those brave Americans who, at this very hour, patrol far-off deserts and distant mountains. They have something to tell us today, just as the fallen heroes who lie in Arlington [the U.S. National Cemetery] whisper through the ages. We honour them not only because they are guardians of our liberty, but because they embody the spirit of service; a willingness to find meaning in something greater than themselves. And yet, at this moment – a moment that will define a generation – it is precisely this spirit that must inhabit us all.

For as much as government can do and must do, it is ultimately the faith and determination of the American people upon which this nation relies. It is the kindness to take in a stranger when the levees break [a reference to Hurrican Katrina, 2005], the selflessness of workers who would rather cut their hours than see a friend lose their job which sees us through our darkest hours. It is the firefighter's courage to storm a stairway filled with smoke [an allusion to the aftermath of the terrorist attack on the World Trade Center on 11 September 2001], but also a parent's willingness to nurture a child, that finally decides our fate.

Our challenges may be new. The instruments with which we meet them may be new. But those values upon which our success depends – hard work and honesty, courage and fair play, tolerance and curiosity, loyalty and patriotism – these things are old. These things are true. They have been the quiet force of progress throughout our history. What is demanded then is a return to these truths. What is required of us now is a new era of responsibility – a recognition, on the part of every American, that we have duties to ourselves, our nation, and the world, duties that we do not grudgingly accept but rather seize gladly, firm in the knowledge that there is nothing so satisfying to the spirit, so defining of our character, than giving our all to a difficult task.

This is the price and the promise of citizenship.

This is the source of our confidence – the knowledge that God calls on us to shape an uncertain destiny.

This is the meaning of our liberty and our creed – why men and women and children of every race and every faith can join in celebration across this magnificent mall [the National Mall in Washington, D.C.], and why a man whose father less than sixty years ago might not have been served at a local restaurant can now stand before you to take a most sacred oath.

So let us mark this day with remembrance, of who we are and how far we have travelled. In the year of America's birth [1776], in the coldest of months, a small band of patriots huddled by dying campfires on the shores of an icy river. The capital was abandoned. The enemy [Britain] was advancing. The snow was stained with blood. At a moment when the outcome of our revolution was most in doubt, the father of our nation [George Washington] ordered these words be read to the people:

'Let it be told to the future world that in the depth of winter, when nothing but hope and virtue could survive, that the city and the country, alarmed at one common danger, came forth to meet it.'

America: in the face of our common dangers, in this winter of our hardship, let us remember these timeless words. With hope and virtue, let us brave once more the icy currents, and endure what storms may come. Let it be said by our children's children that when we were tested we refused to let this journey end, that we did not turn back nor did we falter; and with eyes fixed on the horizon and God's grace upon us, we carried forth that great gift of freedom and delivered it safely to future generations. Thank you. God bless you. And God bless the United States of America.

Acknowledgements

The author and publishers would like to extend their grateful
thanks to http://obamaspeeches.com for its generous help in
compiling this book. All speeches, with the exception of those
listed below, are taken from that site.

p108 US Human Rights Violations: www.ontheissues.org
p114 Second Presidential Debate: www.ontheissues.org
pp124–125 Time Magazine Interview: www.time.com

Photographic credits
Front cover Brooks Kraft/Corbis
p2 Greg Flume/NewSport/Corbis
p6 Jim Young/Reuters/Corbis
p14 Obama for America/Handout/Reuters/Corbis
p18 Brooks Kraft/Corbis
p29 Joe Wrinn/Harvard University/Handout/Corbis
p40 Rick Friedman/Corbis
p47 Brooks Kraft/Corbis
p60 Rune Hellestad/Corbis
p74 Tim Llewellyn/Corbis
p84 Brooks Kraft/Corbis
p90 Tannen Maury/epa/Corbis
p98 Justin Lane/epa/Corbis